Hack Your Job Search

by Jenn Bailey & Tim Condon

Hack Your Job Search

Jenn Bailey & Tim Condon

ISBN: 978-1-950325-80-1

Table of Contents

Book License 7

Before You Begin 9

What You Need 11

Book Source Code & Forums 13

- About the Authors 16
- About the Editors 17

Acknowledgments 19

Introduction 21

- How to Read This Book 22
- What's in Store 22

Section I: Getting Tactical About Your Job Search . 25

Chapter 1: Evaluating Your Options 27

- What You'll Learn 28
- Evaluating Yourself: Are You Ready to Apply for Junior Roles? 28
- Next Step: Are You Ready to Start Sending Out Your Resume? 30
- Deciding Where to Apply 34
- What to Expect During the Interview Process 36
- Conclusion 41
- Key Takeaways 42
- Action Plan 42

Chapter 2: Types of Jobs Available 43

- What You'll Learn 44
- What to Consider When Picking a Role 44
- Deciding on a Company Type 53
- Key Takeaways 55
- Resources 56

Action Plan. 57

Chapter 3: Decoding Job Listings to Find the Right Roles . . . 59
What You'll Learn 60
Exploring Tech Job Titles 60
Determining Which Level to Target. 63
Thinking About Your Future 70
Key Takeaways. 71
Action Plan. 71

Chapter 4: Creating a Resume & Portfolio. 73
What You'll Learn 74
What to Include in Your Resume. 74
What Not to Include in Your Resume 79
Tailoring Resumes. 79
Managing Applicant Tracking Systems 81
Building a Portfolio 82
Crafting a Cover Letter 84
Key Takeaways. 87
Resources. 87
Action Plan. 88

Chapter 5: Traditional & Nontraditional Ways to Find Jobs . 89
What You'll Learn 90
Traditional Versus Nontraditional Ways to Find Jobs 90
Finding a Job Using Hiring Websites 91
Networking 95
Nontraditional Ways to Find Jobs. 102
Following up With Leads 105
Conclusion. 106
Key Takeaways 107
Action Plan 107

Chapter 6: Working With Recruiters. 109

What You'll Learn. 110
How Tech Recruiters Work. 110
How Tech Recruiters Can Help You 111
What to Look for in Recruiters 112
How to Find Software Developer Recruiters 113
How to Interact With Recruiters. 115
Key Takeaways 118
Resources 119
Action Plan 119

Section II: Standing Out From the Crowd 121

Chapter 7: Growing Your Professional Network 123
What You'll Learn. 124
Why Professional Networking is Important. 124
Getting Organized. 126
Finding People to Network With. 129
Networking in Person 131
Networking Online. 133
Maintaining and Growing Your Network. 134
Soft Skills Tips for Networking 135
Key Takeaways 137
Action Plan 137

Chapter 8: Building in Public 139
What You'll Learn. 140
Entering Hackathons and Coding Competitions 140
Coding for the Community 146
Contributing to Open-Source Projects. 147
Shipping Your Own App 150
Sharing Your Accomplishments 151
Conquering Imposter Syndrome 152
Key Takeaways 155

Resources ... 155
Action Plan ... 156

Chapter 9: Learn & Share ... 157
What You'll Learn ... 158
How Learn-and-Share Helps Software Developers ... 158
Selecting a Programming Topic to Learn and Share ... 160
Learning and Sharing With Your Community ... 161
Publishing What You're Learning ... 162
Giving a Technical Presentation ... 167
Teaching and Mentoring Junior Devs ... 169
Key Takeaways ... 171
Resources ... 172
Action Plan ... 172

Chapter 10: What to Do if You're Still Not Landing Interviews ... 173
What You'll Learn ... 174
How to Recognize and Avoid Common Job Application Mistakes ... 174
Gathering and Incorporating Feedback ... 178
Stepping up Your Game ... 179
Managing Your Emotions During a Challenging Job Search ... 181
Sustaining Your Job Search ... 183
Implementing a Continuous Improvement Process for Your Job Search ... 185
Resources ... 186
Key Takeaways ... 186
Action Plan ... 187

Conclusion ... 189

Book License

By purchasing *Hack Your Job Search*, you have the following license:

- You are allowed to use and/or modify the source code in *Hack Your Job Search* in as many apps as you want, with no attribution required.
- You are allowed to use and/or modify all art, images and designs that are included in *Hack Your Job Search* in as many apps as you want, but must include this attribution line somewhere inside your app: "Artwork/images/designs: from *Hack Your Job Search*, available at www.kodeco.com".
- The materials (source code, worksheets, etc.) included in *Hack Your Job Search* is for your personal use only. You are NOT allowed to distribute or sell the materials in *Hack Your Job Search* without prior authorization.
- This book is for your personal use only. You are NOT allowed to reproduce or transmit any part of this book by any means, electronic or mechanical, including photocopying, recording, etc. without previous authorization. You may not sell digital versions of this book or distribute them to friends, coworkers or students without prior authorization. They need to purchase their own copies.

All materials provided with this book are provided on an "as is" basis, without warranty of any kind, express or implied, including but not limited to the warranties of merchantability, fitness for a particular purpose and noninfringement. In no event shall the authors or copyright holders be liable for any claim, damages or other liability, whether in an action of contract, tort or otherwise, arising from, out of or in connection with the software or the use or other dealings in the software.

All trademarks and registered trademarks appearing in this guide are the properties of their respective owners.

Before You Begin

This section tells you a few things you need to know before you get started, such as what you'll need for hardware and software, where to find the project files for this book, and more.

What You Need

To follow along with this book, you'll need the following:

- **A journal**: Throughout this book, you'll reflect on how to grow as a developer and as a candidate and how to put your best self forward. Each chapter ends with an Action Plan, to which you can respond in your journal. Use whatever note-taking system feels right for you and continue with it as you go through your search. It's especially effective to reflect immediately after an interview on what went well and what you felt could have gone better. Then, review these notes before your next interview.
- **A calendar**: You'll use a calendar system, whatever you prefer, to track outreach, networking opportunities and of course, interviews! You may want to set a goal to complete the suggested activities in each chapter by a given date, spreading your work with this book over a period of time. Note this plan down in your calendar and set reminders as well.
- **Perseverance**: More than anything, you need the energy and courage to keep at it. Job hunting can be a long, hard slog. We've each been there, and now we're here for you. As you read through these pages, take what serves you, and know we're cheering you on. You can do this!

Book Source Code & Forums

Where to Download the Materials for This Book

The materials for this book can be cloned or downloaded from the GitHub book materials repository:

- https://github.com/kodecocodes/booh-materials/tree/editions/1.0

Forums

We've also set up an official forum for the book at https://forums.kodeco.com/c/books/hack-your-job-search. This is a great place to ask questions about the book or to submit any errors you may find.

"To all those who have helped me in my career, either directly or indirectly — this one is for you!"

— *Tim Condon*

"To my students and mentees past, present and future. You are the reason I love my career. I wish great prosperity in your journey to you and to those wonderful individuals who mentored me on my path."

— *Jennifer Bailey*

About the Authors

Jennifer Bailey is a former software engineer who is now a full-time professor for Aims Community College in Colorado where she teaches mobile app development for Android and iOS. She also teaches courses in Python, Java, C++, and .NET platform utilizing C#. She is the lead organizer of Google Developer Group of Northern Colorado. She enjoys various Android meetups and conferences around the United States. In her spare time, Jenn enjoys rollerblading, horseback riding and spending time with her teenage daughter, dogs and cats.

Tim Condon is a software developer from Manchester, UK. He runs Broken Hands, a Server-Side Swift consultancy working with clients all over the world. He's also one half of the Vapor Core Team and spends much of his time working on open source and advocating for Swift on the server.

About the Editors

Sandra Grauschopf is the developmental editor of this book. She is also a writer and content strategist as well as the Operational Project Manager for Written Content at Kodeco. She loves to untangle tortured sentences and to travel the world with a trusty book in her hand.

Emily Wydeven is the editor of this book. She's an avid scavenger of typos and grammatical errors and has worked extensively in the tech industry. Emily is a nerd for technology, cats, medical history, and comic books (among many other things). While her favorite comic book characters are Deadpool and Squirrel Girl, the character with whom Emily most closely identifies is Nancy Whitehead.

Susannah Skyer Gupta is the final pass editor for this book. She's an experienced communicator, a veteran of Silicon Valley and a lover of pretty much all things Apple. As someone improving her coding skills later in life, she strongly believes in learning at all ages and making room for everyone in software development. Find Susannah on social media @SuzGupta and listen to her on the Kodeco Season 1 podcast.

Acknowledgments

We would like to thank **Jeff Rames** for coming up with the idea for this book and helping to lay the groundwork for it. We'd also like to thank Adam Rush, Aaron Douglas, Harlan Kellaway, Anu Mittal, Lea Marolt Sonnenschein and Jawwad Ahmad for their efforts and expertise in the job search field.

Introduction

If you're a beginning developer who has just completed a bootcamp, earned a Computer Sciences degree or finished a course of self-taught study, entering the job market with your newly acquired skills might feel daunting. Where do you start? Which companies are right for you? What can you expect to earn?

You're probably aware there's a lot of competition for new developers. According to Statista (https://www.statista.com/statistics/627312/worldwide-developer-population/), the number of software developers in the world is predicted to reach 28.7 million by 2024, an increase of over 4 million new developers since 2020. It's not easy to grab an interviewer's attention in a crowd that big.

Now, imagine that you have experienced mentors who understand exactly where you're coming from, have a great overview of the development landscape and have experience from both sides of the table, as interviewer and interviewee. Best of all, they're willing to take your hand and answer your most pressing questions. That's exactly what this book offers.

Our two authors have a huge amount of experience guiding new developers just like you:

Jenn Bailey is a Kodeco bootcamp mentor and community college professor in the field of computer science. She has coached many students through the process of graduating and finding a job.

Tim Condon brings in the other side of the equation — he's a world-class talent in his field who has recruited and hired a significant number of developers. He knows what it takes to stand out from the crowd and what companies are looking for today.

Together, Jenn and Tim will lead you through the process of landing your first interview. You'll find actionable tips in every chapter so that by the end, you'll have a concrete plan to decide which jobs to apply for and how to impress your interviewers.

Aside from expert tips and advice, each chapter also includes:

- An **action plan** with specific things to do with your new knowledge to advance your job search and to distinguish yourself from other applicants.
- A **worksheet** to help you put your new knowledge to work and track your progress.

How to Read This Book

This book aims to help you focus your job search, prepare all the materials you need and continuously strengthen your abilities and your professional network while you apply for positions. Each chapter of this book builds upon the previous one, especially in Section 1: Getting Tactical About Your Job Search. For this reason, we recommend, especially if you are just starting your search, to read the book straight through initially.

You'll see each chapter concludes with an Action Plan. Build your confidence by challenging yourself to perform the listed actions. You can also find a link to a corresponding worksheet in each chapter. Work through this material to motivate yourself to take action and apply your newly acquired knowledge.

You might want to return to certain chapters, parts of chapters or worksheets as you go through the process, including after taking breaks to refocus.

What's in Store

This book is split into two main sections:

Section I: Getting Tactical About Your Job Search

The first section of this book focuses on practical steps you can take to find the right software developer job for you. In this section, you'll find chapters that cover a variety of topics to help you make informed decisions about your job search.

Chapter 1, "Evaluating Your Options", covers key considerations for determining if you have the necessary skills and experience to start applying for software developer jobs.

Chapter 2, "Types of Jobs Available", provides an overview of the different types of software developer roles and the skills and experience they typically require.

Chapter 3, "Decoding Job Listings to Find the Right Roles", offers guidance on how to research the job market and identify companies and job opportunities that align with your values and needs.

Chapter 4, "Creating a Resume & Portfolio", provides tips on how to create a standout resume and portfolio that will impress potential employers.

Chapter 5, "Traditional & Nontraditional Ways to Find Jobs," explores a range of job search strategies, including networking, online job boards and job fairs.

Chapter 6, "Working With Recruiters," discusses the pros and cons of working with a recruiter and provides tips for building a successful relationship with a recruiter.

"Getting Tactical About Your Job Search" is designed to provide you with the tools and knowledge you need to confidently and effectively navigate the job search process and land your first software developer interview.

Section II: Standing Out From the Crowd

The second half of this book focuses on helping you differentiate yourself from other job candidates and make a strong impression on potential employers.

Chapter 7, "Growing Your Professional Network", explores the importance of networking and provides tips for expanding your network of contacts in the tech industry.

Chapter 8, "Building in Public", discusses the benefits of sharing your work and expertise publicly through blogs, social media and other platforms.

Chapter 9, "Learn & Share", offers advice on how to continuously learn and improve your skills, as well as how to share your knowledge with others through mentoring, teaching and public speaking.

Chapter 10, "What to Do if You're Still Not Landing Interviews", provides guidance on what to do if you're struggling to land interviews despite your best efforts. It covers common reasons why job seekers may not be getting interviews and offers strategies for addressing those challenges.

Overall, “Standing Out From the Crowd” is designed to help you stand out from other job candidates and increase your chances of success in the competitive world of tech job hunting.

We hope that you’ll enjoy this book and that it will help you land your dream job interview. If you have any questions or feedback, please visit our forum. We’re looking forward to hearing from you!

Section I: Getting Tactical About Your Job Search

The first section of this book focuses on practical steps you can take to find the right mobile developer job for you. In this section, you'll find chapters that cover a variety of topics to help you make informed decisions about your job search.

"Getting Tactical About Your Job Search" is designed to provide you with the tools and knowledge you need to confidently and effectively navigate the job search process and land your first interview in the industry.

Chapter 1: Evaluating Your Options

By Tim Condon

So, you've just finished a coding bootcamp, university or a self-taught learning path. Congratulations on learning a new set of skills! Whether you want to improve your financial situation, work for your dream company or find a job you love starting each morning, breaking into the technology industry can change your life. However, you're probably asking some big questions: Are your programming skills enough to get you a new job? And where should you even start looking? This chapter will help you make those decisions.

What You'll Learn

In this chapter, you'll go over some factors to consider before applying for your first job. You'll start by asking yourself some important questions to see if you're ready, professionally and personally, to begin applying and to help you take your first steps toward landing a job.

> **Note:** This book's GitHub materials repository contains a worksheet for each chapter. Be sure to take the time to write down the answers to these questions. Actually writing them out forces you to give these questions the attention they deserve, and in the process, you'll create an action plan that you'll refer to throughout the interview process.

It's hard to be introspective! However, these steps are essential to ensuring you're applying to the right places — and that you'll be successful when you do.

Along the way, you'll learn:

- The skills and knowledge companies expect you to have when applying for your first role.
- How to decide when to start sending out resumes.
- Important job aspects to consider, such as your financial needs and the types of companies you want to target.
- The different stages of a job application.

Evaluating Yourself: Are You Ready to Apply for Junior Roles?

It's not unusual to feel a little lost when a course of study ends. When you're working on a degree or going through a bootcamp, you have a course laid out for you. When you graduate, you're left on your own to work out your next steps. Are you really ready to get a job? Especially after an accelerated course like a bootcamp, you might not be sure.

Don't worry — no company expects a junior dev to know everything. You won't be expected to build an iOS app, an Android app, the back end, the database and the website *and* scale the project to millions of users. ;] Instead, companies are looking for junior devs with a lot of promise. Passion and dedication will go a long way toward getting your first mobile dev role.

When I hire developers, both junior *and* senior, the main thing I'm looking for is the **ability to learn**. Tech is a never-ending cycle of change. Whether it's moving from Objective-C to Swift, Java to Kotlin, or back end to front end, you'll need to pick up new things throughout your career. Demonstrating a willingness to work out new problems, seek out answers and just try stuff out will go further than any other trait.

Remember, companies won't expect people applying to junior roles to have much experience. You won't need to have apps with millions of users in the App Store, for example. Most people start their tech careers in junior roles with no professional experience.

In an interview, you might be asked to demonstrate some coding knowledge or the basics of building an app — but you don't need to know everything. Having a portfolio of things you've tried, like cornerstone projects from your bootcamp or sample apps you've created from Kodeco videos or books, is a great start. Showcasing open-source contributions is another good way to demonstrate an eagerness to learn.

> **Note**: See Chapter 4, "Creating a Resume & Portfolio", and Chapter 8, "Building in Public", for more information on how to help yourself stand out as a junior developer.

So, which skills *should* you be able to demonstrate as a junior developer? Next, you'll cover some of the knowledge interviewers are likely to look for in a junior dev.

Required Skills for Beginner Developer Roles

Companies expect any developer, even at a junior level, to have basic programming skills. You'll be expected to know **common programming terms** like `for` loops, **conditional statements** (`if/else`) and how to **build and run** apps.

If you're applying for a web developer role, you should be able to create a **basic website** and run it in your browser. If you're applying for a mobile developer role, you should know how to **create a simple app** and run it on a simulator.

To stand out from your fellow developers a bit, it's useful to know:

- How to use a source control management system like Git (https://www.kodeco.com/books/git-apprentice) to store your code.
- A basic understanding of HTTP and how to send requests to an API.
- How to write and run tests (https://www.kodeco.com/books/ios-test-driven-development-by-tutorials).

Don't worry too much about specific technologies — most concepts are transferable. For instance, if you've learned Android development and are applying for a junior iOS developer role, don't worry about not being an expert in the Swift language. You should, however, familiarize yourself with building a basic iOS app using Xcode because that's the preferred IDE. If you'd like to brush up on your skills, check out our iOS and Swift for Beginners Learning Path (https://www.kodeco.com/ios/paths/learn).

And if you've learned iOS and are applying for an Android role, work through a getting started tutorial to see how Android Studio works. Our Android and Kotlin for Beginners (https://www.kodeco.com/android/paths/learn) learning path is a good candidate.

To reiterate: Companies won't expect you to be language experts or wizards at creating UIs. Make sure you have a solid foundation in your role's basic skills, and the rest will follow.

Job descriptions usually list expected skills, so you can use them as a checklist to see what you know and where there's room for improvement. However, as mentioned earlier, don't be put off if you don't have every "required" skill listed. Sometimes, the job descriptions are a little overbearing. If you feel solid with the basics, you'll be fine.

Next Step: Are You Ready to Start Sending Out Your Resume?

The first step toward deciding if you're ready is to work out when to start applying. Just because you've graduated doesn't mean you have to send out applications instantly! You have a choice: Should you apply now, or should you spend some time proving your skills to potential employers?

If you have money to cover your living costs while you build a portfolio, a delay might be worthwhile. However, applying to many different jobs gives you invaluable experience with the interview process. This can help you learn which jobs feel right to you and give you interviewing skills to improve your chances of landing the right job.

Neither decision is wrong — just work out what's best for you and try it. Most important, however, is to set a timeline and stick with it. Don't let imposter syndrome or nervousness prevent you from getting started! The Chapter 1 Worksheet (https://github.com/kodecocodes/booh-materials/blob/editions/1.0/01-evaluating-your-options/Chapter01Worksheet.pdf) will help you make a timeline that works best for you.

If you're not sure which path is right, here are some of the advantages and disadvantages of jumping into the job hunt versus getting everything lined up before you start.

Applying Right Away

The best way to get better at interviewing and applying for jobs is through experience. And the best way to get that experience is by going through the process, seeing how you get on and improving based on the feedback you receive.

In software, there's the concept of an **MVP**, or minimum viable product. This philosophy says it's impossible to know what your users want until you ship your app and get feedback. So, you don't try to put out a perfect app; instead, you start with one that works, then refine it based on user feedback until it meets your customers' actual needs.

The same principle applies to finding a job. Until you get experience with tailoring resumes for different roles and going through interviews, it's hard to know where you need to improve. So, it could be useful to start applying sooner rather than later to gain that experience.

The most important thing to do as you go through each interview is **ask for feedback**. Most companies will give you feedback on your application and interview performance, especially if you ask. Use their feedback to find out where you have room to improve.

Another important reason to start applying immediately is that the hiring process takes time. According to data from the Higher Education Statistics Agency (https://www.hesa.ac.uk/data-and-analysis/graduates/releases), most computing graduates end up in full-time employment... eventually. (Outcomes in the following chart do not add to 100% due to rounding.)

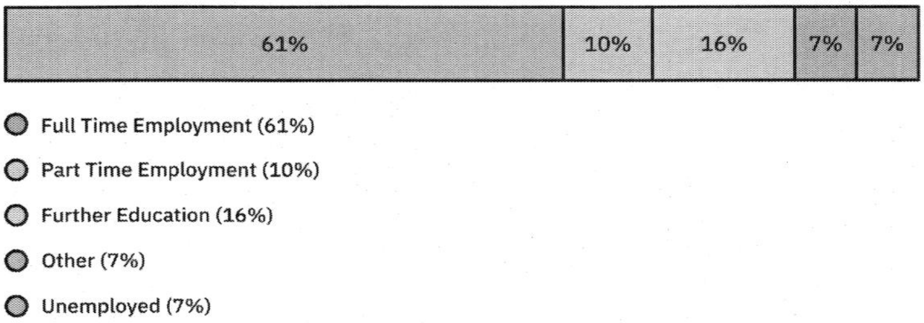

https://www.hesa.ac.uk/data-and-analysis/sb263/figure-10

Nearly all computing grads end up employed. You will too.

But it doesn't happen overnight. The average interview process takes almost 49 days, according to LinkedIn's Economic Graph team (https://www.linkedin.com/pulse/can-you-wait-49-days-why-getting-hired-takes-so-long-george-anders/). And that doesn't consider the time it takes to find jobs to apply to, or the gap between accepting an offer and starting in your role.

Especially in an ever-changing economic environment, landing a job takes time. And if your savings are dwindling, those delays can put a lot of pressure on you. So, the earlier you start applying, the more quickly you're likely to find gainful employment.

Taking Time to Apply

By applying as soon as you think your skills are ready, you shorten how long you have to wait before starting a job, and you improve your interviewing skills. So, when might you want to **not** apply right away? Next, you'll look at three situations where you might want to hold off:

1. When applying for your dream job.
2. When you struggle with rejection.
3. When you've identified weaknesses you want to work on.

Waiting Before Applying for Your Dream Job

Applying right away when you're targeting your **dream job** might hurt your chances. Repeatedly applying for the same role at the same company and getting rejected will count against you, so it's good to be well prepared before sending in your resume.

First, perfect your application and read up on the company's interview process. Chapter 4, "Creating a Resume & Portfolio", explains how to create a great application.

Additionally, you can prepare yourself to give the best interview possible. Focus on gaining more skills and improving your application process. If you have time, take a few months to concentrate on building your portfolio to put you ahead of the field. See Section II, "Standing Out From the Crowd", for specific ideas.

A good middle ground might be to start applying for jobs that you're not sure you'll love, and hold off on applying for those dream companies. That way, you'll gain interview experience while using the extra time to work on your portfolio. And who knows, you might luck out and land a job at a company that's better than you expected.

Avoiding Rejection by Targeting Your Applications

If you know you have a hard time dealing with rejection, you can consider targeting the jobs you apply to more carefully. Take the time to get your resume just right, polish your presentation skills and mindfully select the roles you apply for.

However, don't let a fear of rejection discourage you. Remind yourself that getting turned down is just part of the job application process. It might help to think of every "no" as getting you one step closer to your eventual acceptance.

You can also take the time after each rejection to reflect on the process. What went well? What can you improve next time? Each rejection provides you with vital experience to help you get to a positive result.

That said, be careful not to fall into the trap of spending so much time preparing that you don't actually apply. Take the same attitude as when you prepare to ship your MVP: You don't have to be perfect to get started. It's better to get a rejection than not to apply at all!

Addressing Weaknesses in Your Skill Set

If you've inventoried your skills and realized that you have some weaknesses you want to address, it makes sense to put off applying for a short time while you work on them. This could mean following along with some tutorials to improve your programming skills or doing some mock interviews (https://www.kodeco.com/34421990-mock-interview-techniques-for-tech-job-searchers) to improve your interview techniques.

That said, don't be afraid to apply for roles that seem out of reach. Unfortunately, many companies post job openings with unrealistic requirements, especially if these postings come from recruiters.

According to research by global staffing firm Robert Half (https://www.prnewswire.com/news-releases/survey-42-percent-of-job-applicants-dont-meet-skills-requirements-but-companies-are-willing-to-train-up-300813540.html), 84% of companies say they'd be willing to train a good candidate that doesn't meet every requirement of a role.

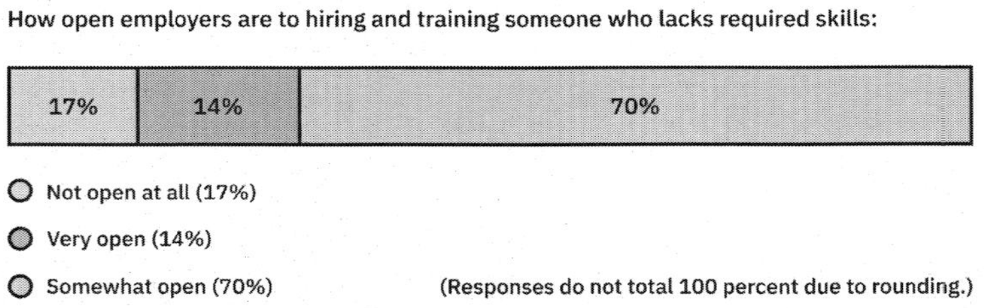

Apply even if you're missing some skills. Most employers will train you.

So, if you see a role you really like and think you'd be good at, don't be afraid to apply. The worst that can happen is they say no!

Deciding Where to Apply

Once you decide that you're ready to apply, you need to decide which companies to target. As a junior developer, you have a wide variety of options available to you, which can also make it difficult to decide where to start.

So next, you'll learn some of the factors to consider when determining which companies you want to apply to, including:

- Whether a large or small company is better for you.
- Which tech stack the company uses.
- The compensation package the company offers.

Company Size

All types of companies need developers these days, which means that you can apply to tiny start-ups and huge multinational corporations. With some exceptions, the size of a company determines a lot about its culture and the opportunities you'll receive there.

To look at the ends of the spectrum, here are some advantages and disadvantages of startups versus big corporations:

- **Start-ups**: Start-ups offer a dynamic environment where you're able to have a big impact on the company. You'll probably get to work in lots of different areas of technology. Start-ups are fast-moving companies with big opportunities, and they call for people who are flexible and motivated. However, they're also risky. Oftentimes, they don't have a lot of revenue, so salaries might be lower and benefits less generous. There's also a risk that they'll go out of business, sometimes without ever even creating a marketable product.
- **Large Companies**: In larger companies, you could have the opportunity to work on products that millions of people use. The pace is usually slower, there's more stability and the company is less likely to be constantly in flux. Many large companies also have a larger tech team, which means more opportunities for mentorship. However, there's usually more bureaucracy and fewer opportunities to take a leadership role and to try new things.

Most people prefer one kind of company over the other, so it's worth considering what's best for you — or if you're really looking for something in the middle. Chapter 2, "Types of Jobs Available", covers this in more detail.

Tech Stack

The technology you work on has a big impact on your work life. For example, if you're applying for an iOS role and want to write Swift apps, make sure the company uses Swift. If the company uses React Native and Xamarin and you want to write native apps, then you're not going to enjoy your job.

To determine if the tech stack of a company is one you want to work with, check the job description and ask lots of technology questions during your interviews.

You should also see how modern the company's tech stack is. Do they migrate to new features quickly so you'll get to use the latest syntax and frameworks? Or do they use custom tools that are different from what you're used to?

There are pros and cons to any approach, so make sure you find out and consider what you want to work on.

Compensation & Benefits

When you consider the compensation you're looking for, it's natural to think primarily about the salary. However, it's important to consider the entire benefits package when you're looking for the right job to apply to.

There's a wide range of salaries out there, with most of the highest paying roles based in Silicon Valley in the United States. However, many of the locations that pay best also have high costs of living. And that's even assuming you want to move at all.

So, when you evaluate a job description to determine if you want to apply for a role, look at all the benefits. This not only includes salary but also things like whether you can work remotely, the amount of vacation time, training budgets, parental leave, stock options and so on. Chapter 3, "Decoding Job Listings to Find the Right Roles", covers this in more detail.

What to Expect During the Interview Process

Now that you've decided when and where you want to apply, it's worth taking a moment to familiarize yourself with the typical tech interview process. Many people find the different stages of applying for a job intimidating — but you don't have to be one of them.

It helps to understand the purpose of each interview stage... and to remember that interviewing offers a good chance for *you* to interview the company as well.

Companies use different processes for hiring employees depending on their size and needs. The most common interview stages you'll encounter on your journey to become a developer include:

- CV/resume submission
- Telephone interview
- Culture-fit interview
- Whiteboard interview
- Pair programming exercise
- Take-home project
- Assessment centers

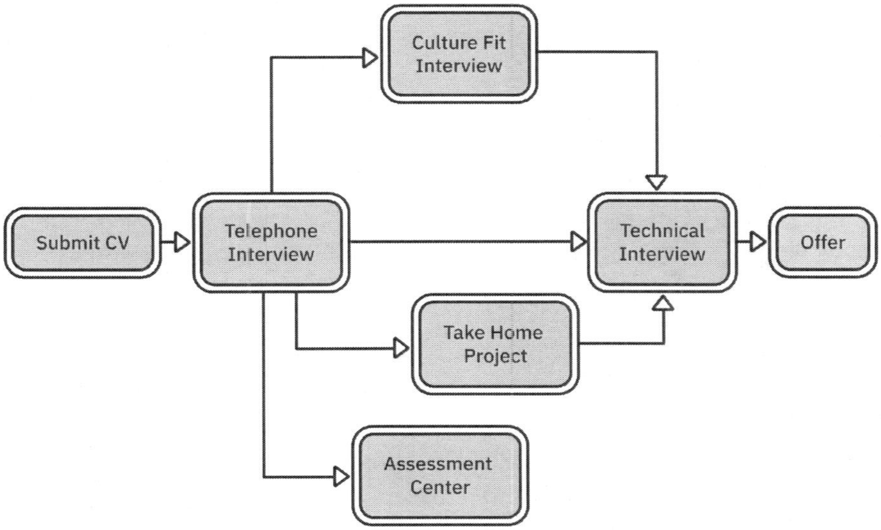

Sometimes, there are many stages to pass. Other times, you can get an offer after a single interview.

> **Note**: Keep in mind that not all companies use all of these interview stages. Smaller companies tend to do an interview that covers technical aspects, culture fit and your resume all at once. There might be a follow-up interview or two, but often you'll receive an offer or rejection letter after just one interview.

Submitting Your Resume

Almost all job applications require you to start with some form of resume. This might be a copy of a traditional resume or an application form on the company's website that breaks down your experience into education, job history and so on.

Some applications also require a cover letter explaining why you want to work for that company, what makes you interested in the role and why you'd be a good fit.

See Chapter 4, "Creating a Resume & Portfolio", for more information.

Telephone Screening

Often, the first step for larger companies with more hiring stages is a telephone screening (https://www.kodeco.com/34440170-effective-phone-screen-interview-tactics-for-mobile-developers) to determine if you're fit for the role.

This interview covers your resume and experience, along with some basic questions to gauge your knowledge. It may be conducted by someone with a technical background or by a non-technical person from human resources or another branch of the company.

Culture-Fit Interview

In the culture-fit interview, you'll meet with a potential manager or colleague to see if you'll get along well with the team.

For example, if you're applying for a customer-facing role, can you articulate problems in a simple way? If you're applying for a web developer role, do you have a passion for design? If the role involves working in open source, are you comfortable working in public and interacting with a community?

Remember, interviews are two-way processes. They are as much about seeing if *you* like the company as they are if the company likes you. Be sure to take full advantage of this opportunity. A role that looks great on paper might not be the right fit for you. Take the opportunity of face-to-face time to ask as many questions as you like. The culture-fit interview is a good time to make sure you get along with your prospective manager, for example.

An important question to ask is, are the people you'll work with passionate about what they're working on, or do they seem not to enjoy it? If they don't enjoy their jobs, it's likely you won't either.

You can ask questions about how well you'll fit in with the company as well as technical questions. For example, you could ask:

- Do you host social events so colleagues can get to know one another?
- What is the tech stack like?
- How will your day-to-day routine look?
- What is the turnover rate at the company?

Once you've worked out what's important to you in your job, you can ensure you're applying for a job that meets those needs.

Technical Interviews

The **technical interview** gives you the chance to demonstrate your technical prowess. There are three major types of technical interviews:

- Whiteboard interviews
- Pair programming exercises
- Take-home projects

In a **whiteboard interview**, you're asked to draw algorithms, code or solutions on a whiteboard in front of the interviewers. The industry is moving away from this kind of interview because they put a lot of pressure on people. Furthermore, you're typically asked about computer science questions that aren't relevant to your job. However, it's a good idea to prepare for this kind of interview, in case you want to interview with a company that still uses them.

Pair programming is where you're asked to write code to solve a particular problem, and you have another person to talk to. You can bounce ideas off your pair, ask them questions, and discuss your solution.

The aim of pair programming interviews is to replicate your potential job as closely as possible and to see how you work and get along with people. You're usually allowed to look up questions and solutions, but be prepared to explain why you're using that piece of code from Stack Overflow and what it does!

In a **take-home project**, you'll be given a well-defined problem to solve in your own time. For example, you might have to write an app that reads from a specific API then displays the results in a table.

Take-home projects are popular because they give people time to work through the problem without the pressure of working live. The best companies will even pay you for the time the project takes.

The project doesn't need to be perfect, but you should be prepared to explain your code in the interview. For example, your interviewers might ask why you chose to use a particular framework or UI element. Remember, there's no one right answer; the interviewers are simply trying to understand your thought processes.

The project is partly used as a simple screening exercise and partly to have something to discuss. You don't have to spend weeks on it; you should stick to the time guidelines they give you.

Most technical interviews will ask you questions relevant to your role. You might be asked about language features or your experience with using particular dependencies. These interviews probe your knowledge, but remember, you won't be expected to know everything as a junior developer. Don't be afraid to give a wrong answer or to say that you'd need to research that problem.

It's OK to **ask for clarification.** If you don't know an answer, explain the parts that you do know and describe what you'd do to find out the rest. You can even ask if you can look it up to explain it. That comes across much better than trying to make something up — it's easy for your interviewer to tell when you bluff.

Visiting an Assessment Center

Finally, very large companies might use **assessment centers**. These are all-day, or even multiple-day, events where you'll have technical interviews, culture-fit interviews, team exercises in an all-in-one compressed session. These tend to be used by non-technical companies recruiting for generic roles or by universities for graduate program admissions, but you may encounter them in your developer interview process.

Research the interview styles the companies you apply to use so you won't be surprised. You should be told what the interview will involve when you're invited; if you're unsure, it's always best to ask. This shows an interest in the role and willingness to prepare while also ensuring you have time to prepare yourself.

Conclusion

This chapter covers a lot of information you need to take your first step toward getting a job in tech. It's hard to process everything on the first go, so go back over the different sections if you need to.

Assessing yourself, working out what your skills are and if you *feel* ready is not an easy job. It takes time to pull everything together — and that's OK. It's a useful process to undertake, and it will set you up nicely for the rest of the book.

Remember, junior developers aren't expected to have lots of experience. Companies usually want to see a willingness to learn and an ability to find answers to your problems. Making sure you can demonstrate an interest in technology and your desired field is far more important than having 10 apps in the App Store.

Key Takeaways

- Before you start applying, take some time for self-evaluation to determine your skills, which companies are right for you and what your timeframe needs to be.
- Different companies have different interview processes. Get to know the different types of interviews. Ask which ones the company will use when you're invited to interview.
- Remember that, no matter what the company asks for in its job posting, you don't need to be a perfect fit or have all the knowledge. Remember that a solid foundation in the basics, eagerness to learn and the ability to cooperate with your coworkers are more important traits than any specific language knowledge.

Action Plan

You should now have some understanding of what you need to think about before applying for your first role. Before you apply, you should:

- **Write down the skills** that you currently have to evaluate if you need more time before applying.
- **Prepare a list** of things you must have in your job and a list of nice-to-haves.
- Use this list to **work out the type of company and job** you want to target.
- **Research the interview process** for the company you're applying to.
- Put together a **list of things you'll need** before applying, like a resume.
- **Read any relevant chapters** in the rest of the book!

> **Reflect on what you've learned**: Find this chapter's worksheet (PDF (https://github.com/kodecocodes/booh-materials/blob/editions/1.0/01-evaluating-your-options/Chapter01Worksheet.pdf)) in this book's GitHub materials repo.

Chapter 2: Types of Jobs Available

By Tim Condon

Getting into the tech industry sounds like a solid goal. But once you get closer to actually applying for a job, you realize that you have a lot of options — which means that you also have to make a lot of decisions. Even as a junior dev, you'll choose among a wide variety of roles, areas of expertise and types of companies to work for.

To help you make a choice that works for you, you need to consider what you want from your career and what brings you satisfaction in a job. This chapter will give you a solid start.

What You'll Learn

In this chapter, you'll narrow down your potential job search from "a role in tech" to a specific job position and type of company. Along the way, you'll learn:

- What kinds of tech roles are available today.
- How company size affects your search.
- Which perks to prioritize.
- How to evaluate a company's culture and technologies.

It's time to get started!

What to Consider When Picking a Role

Now that you know some of the options available to you in tech, you can start thinking about the direction you want to follow. There are a few steps to deciding what you need out of a job. The first step, as described above, is to think about which roles match your personality and make you feel excited about working in them. However, there are some additional considerations as well.

These considerations include:

- The type of dev role that suits you best.
- How well different roles pay.
- The culture at the companies you're applying to.
- The perks each role offers.

Next, you'll learn more about each of these considerations. And then it will be time to look at which companies will be able to meet these goals.

Before you can apply for a position, you need to decide what type of developer you want to be. When getting into tech, you'll likely start at a junior level, but you might be surprised to realize you have options beyond simply being a "software developer". Software development itself includes several subcategories, and there are also roles like data scientist, site reliability engineer (SRE), test engineer, infrastructure developer — the list goes on!

To help you narrow your focus, you'll start by learning about some common roles for people entering the tech job market.

Software Engineering

When most people start thinking about a role in tech, they're usually visualizing a role as a **software engineer** or **software developer**. Software developers (hopefully!) spend most of their day writing code, whether that means creating mobile apps for consumers or building APIs (application programming interfaces) for mobile apps to consume.

Some of the different roles in software development include:

Front-end Developer

Builds websites and web applications for browsers.

- **Important skills**: The day-to-day work usually involves writing JavaScript or TypeScript. For this role, you'll need to know at least some HTML, CSS and web design principles. You may also work closely with a design team to build websites.
- **Best suited to**: Someone who enjoys design and building things where you get an instant visual reward.

Mobile Developer

Works on apps for mobile devices like phones, tablets and wearables.

- **Important skills**: Generally, you'll use a programming language like Swift or Kotlin or a cross-platform framework like Flutter or React Native.
- **Best suited to**: A developer who enjoys designing and making apps for mobile devices.

Back-end Engineer

Creates APIs for apps to use. This role gives you a lot variety in the technologies you'll use because most languages support building APIs. Be sure to discuss tech stack choices when you interview for back-end engineer positions. Depending on a company's size, you might work closely with the front-end engineers who use the APIs you build.

- **Important skills**: When you build back-end apps, you need to consider how to run and deploy them. Therefore, it's useful to know something about AWS (Amazon Web Services) and Google Cloud. You should also have a good understanding of HTTP and sending and receiving API requests.
- **Best suited to**: People who enjoy working with projects that have several moving parts and who are interested in server technologies and learning how to deal with large numbers of users.

Full-stack Developer

Covers both front-end and back-end development, as well as additional responsibilities like managing infrastructure. Most companies have different roles for front- and back-end development, but smaller companies might ask you to do a bit of everything.

- **Important skills**: You'll need to understand the differences between front-end and back-end development and how they fit together. You should be able to learn how to apply your skills to a number of different areas.
- **Best suited to**: People who are looking for variety and responsibility and enjoy learning different technologies. People who enjoy smaller company environments where they have a wider impact.

Library Developer

Builds libraries and SDKs (software development kits) for other developers to use. In this role, you'll work closely with other developers and have the satisfaction of knowing that lots of different teams use the libraries you build.

- **Important skills**: You should have experience using existing libraries and SDKs so you know how to make your own projects useful. You need to be able to communicate with other developers to find out what they need and be good at writing technical documentation.
- **Best suited to**: People who enjoy having fellow developers rather than end users as customers. People who enjoy writing code that other people will use.

Each role has different responsibilities and day-to-day tasks. If you enjoy creating beautiful apps for users, then front-end or mobile development is for you. If you really enjoy working with other developers, library development is a good choice.

Some of these roles are user-facing, meaning you'll be building directly for consumers. It's really rewarding to see that someone sitting next to you at a coffee shop is using the app you built! Likewise, building APIs and seeing how many people use your code every hour is a great feeling.

But software development is just the tip of the iceberg when it comes to roles in tech. There are other types of positions you might consider applying for as well.

Data Engineering

Data engineers focus on collecting, storing and analyzing data to help a business make informed decisions. This might involve working out why product sales spike at certain times of the year or trying to predict how changing your website will affect site traffic.

Data engineering relies heavily on math, so you'll need a good understanding of statistics for the role. Knowledge of machine learning is also useful to help you automate repetitive tasks, predict future occurrences and find trends in the data.

- **Important skills**: Statistics and mathematics are important for this role. You should have some knowledge of tools used to analyze data and how to interpret the results.
- **Best suited to**: People who like numbers, experiments and discerning patterns from data.

Test Engineering

The traditional view of software testing involves groups of people following a spreadsheet to manually check different parts of an app. These days, however, things are very different!

Dedicated test engineers, also known as quality assurance or QA engineers, help automate testing. This lets them find problems more quickly, test more areas of the app and release fixes faster.

Test engineers build tooling to help run tests for their teams, then work closely with developers to see how best to test the apps.

- **Important skills**: You should have experience testing frameworks and writing tests for mobile devices, networks or websites. You should also know how to write scripts to help automate testing.
- **Best suited to**: Folks who like exploring and breaking things!

Infrastructure Engineering

Modern software is so complex that there is a tech role dedicated to building and deploying apps that are reliable and work flawlessly for users around the world.

Infrastructure engineers, or site reliability engineers (SREs), are responsible for working out how to release apps. For example, SREs build tooling to make global deployments simpler, work with developers to ensure that apps scale to meet demand and create strategies to handle entire data centers going offline. You may also hear this role referred to as DevOps, short for developer operations.

Site reliability engineers historically work at larger companies, but many smaller companies are starting to incorporate SREs into their teams.

- **Important skills**: You need to be able to write scripts and automate many aspects of deploying and monitoring apps and sites. You should be willing to learn how to deploy apps, keep them secure and ensure they don't break.
- **Best suited to**: People who want to work in larger organizations and who are interested in the lower levels of technology like networking and hardware.

Developer Relations

Developer relations, or DevRel for short, is a common role in companies that make products for other developers. A DevRel's goal is to deeply understand their own products so they can showcase how they work to the developers who need them.

DevRels present at conferences and field questions from developers on how to use their products. Because the role involves creating videos and writing tutorials and blog posts, it's useful to have strong writing and presentation skills.

This job suits someone who enjoys a lot of variety in their work life. They often find themselves in situations where they don't know exactly which products or SDKs might fill a potential customer's needs, making this a great role for someone who likes investigating solutions.

- **Important skills**: Content creation, including writing, coding sample apps and filming and editing videos. Willingness and ability to travel to conferences and present talks. Being able to present new technologies in different ways that others will understand.
- **Best suited to**: People who enjoy creating content, exploring new technologies and teaching and engaging with other developers.

Other Roles

The list above is just a sample of the roles you can pursue in technology. There are lots of others! Cybersecurity engineers ensure that products are secure. Database administrators (DBAs) make databases that are quick and efficient. There are network engineers, platform developers, machine learning experts and many more. For any field that interests you, there's probably a role that focuses on that area.

If that feels overwhelming, don't worry. You'll probably move around roles as you progress in your career, so you don't have to stress about finding the one that's perfect for you at the beginning. Once you have your foot in the door, it's much easier to switch.

When looking for a particular role, make sure you read the job description carefully to see if it involves what you want to work on. For example, if you're looking for a mobile developer role, check to see whether you'll work with native technologies or a cross-platform framework because those are two very different experiences.

Keep in mind, you can also pursue jobs that are based on research and not development. Research involves a lot of exploration, which is great for curious minds. It's exciting to try and make things work! However, the work you do might never be seen outside of your team.

That said, programmers who work in research fields provide essential expertise to the wider academic community. For example, bioinformatics programmers at SRI International developed the Pathway Tools in the BioCyc Genome Database Collection. Now, they help scientists learn more about metabolic networks. If you're expert in a field in addition to computing, using your programming skills to improve research in that field could be a satisfying challenge.

Which Roles Pay Best?

One important consideration, of course, is how much you'll earn in different roles. If you're undecided about the path you want to take, choosing one that pays better is a smart decision. However, it's important to remember that salaries are likely to be lower and less varied between different roles when you start out.

Occupation	2021	Change from 2020
IT Management CEO, CIO, CTO, VP, Dir.	$151,983	△ 6.0%
Systems Architect	$147,901	△ 5.1%
Cloud Architect/Engineer	$140,571	△ 3.0%
Cyber Security Engineer/Architect	$135,059	△ 0.5%
Data Architect*	$128,835	▽ 3.2%
Business/Management Consultant	$126,531	△ 4.0%
Program Analyst/Manager	$123,755	△ 0.8%
Data Scientist*	$120,650	△ 0.6%
Product Manager	$120,323	▽ 0.2%
Software Developer	$120,204	△ 8.0%
Devops Engineer*	$119,201	△ 3.5%
MIS Manager	$119,186	▽ 1.0%
Project Manager	$118,517	△ 1.4%
Data Engineer	$117,295	▽ 1.1%
Systems Engineer	$112,407	▽ 0.8%
Database Administrator	$111,362	△ 12.4%
Cybersecurity Analyst	$102,253	▽ 0.8%
Business Analyst/Intelligence Analyst	$101,497	△ 4.0%
UX/UI Designer*	$101,260	△ 10.1%
Web Developer	$98,912	△ 21.3%
Computer/Mainframe Programmer*	$97,320	△ 6.5%
QA Engineer/Tester	$93,932	△ 4.9%
Network Engineer	$93,373	△ 2.0%
Systems Analyst	$93,278	△ 5.5%
Application Support Engineer	$91,176	△ 1.3%
Systems Administrator	$88,642	△ 6.2%
Data Analyst	$84,779	△ 11.5%

Average tech salaries in 2021.

According to a report from Dice on tech salaries (https://www.dice.com/technologists/ebooks/tech-salary-report/salary-trends/), the top-paying jobs are cybersecurity engineers and data scientists — roles that require specialized expertise. These aren't likely to be jobs that you'll land fresh out of a bootcamp or course of study, but you might want to consider directing future goals in that direction.

Levels.fyi is a good site to find out average salaries for roles, companies and locations. However, be sure to work out what your total compensation package is before making a decision. Many companies offer stock options with different vesting periods on top of salaries, and other benefits, like being able to work from home, make a big difference, too.

Considering a Company's Industry, Culture and Perks

The same role can feel very different depending on where you work; a good culture fit can make the difference between loving and hating your job. That's why financial compensation is only one part of job satisfaction; you also need to consider other aspects, like feeling that you're doing something worthwhile and a company culture that helps you thrive.

First, imagine the kind of positive impact you'd like to have in your job. This could mean working on clean energy technology to combat climate change or developing an app to bring your local community together. Or it might mean working for a company with millions of users, knowing that your work will have a big impact. Everyone is different, so think about what you envision bringing you satisfaction in your job.

> **Tip**: For a rubric about how to quantify what's important for you in a company, see Jeff Rames' article, How to Decide If a Company Is Right for You (https://www.kodeco.com/36309982-evaluating-job-offers-how-to-decide-if-a-company-is-right-for-you).

In terms of company culture, think about what makes you respect a company and enjoy working for them more. Some non-technical company core values you might want to consider include:

- **Remote or in-office**: The COVID-19 pandemic has changed working forever, especially in tech. Many people are choosing to work remotely to give them greater flexibility to live where they want, spend more time with their family and friends and stop commuting. Others enjoy a greater sense of teamwork from working with their colleagues in person. Especially as a beginner developer, meeting your mentors face-to-face on a daily basis can be helpful. You'll need to think about this and decide which work environment is right for you.
- **Commitment to diversity**: Does the company understand the value of hiring people from a broad variety of backgrounds? Do they demonstrate diversity in their senior leadership?
- **Placing value on fun**: Work and fun don't have to be diametrically opposed. Some companies recognize that a workplace that values fun as well as hard work fosters better morale and less burnout.
- **Good work/life balance**: The days of all-night coding sessions just to keep your job are over. Does the company respect its employees as people, offering flexible and reasonable working hours and a generous (or unlimited) vacation policy?

Perks to Consider

Software developers are always in short supply, so many companies offer juicy perks to entice good devs to work for them. This could be free meals at the office or free laundry. There might be an onsite gym for you to use, foosball tables or even nap pods. These perks shouldn't be your main focus, but they might help you decide between similar offers.

There are many aspects of company culture to consider, so working out what matters to you is an important step. For example, when I last looked for a job, I wrote a list of qualities I wanted in my next role. Some of the qualities I was looking for in the company included:

- **Data-driven**: Should A/B test all features, gather metrics about performance and use these to determine their direction.
- **Engineering based**: Have a solid engineering foundation. Use Agile best practices such as test-driven development and pair programming.

- **Learning-oriented**: Have an opportunity to attend conferences, go on training courses and share knowledge with colleagues.
- **Transparent**: Be open with customers and within the company. Allow dialogs and conversations. Let everyone question everything.
- **Automated**: Spend time developing tools to deploy and release as quickly as possible, as often as possible.
- **User-oriented**: Provide a great user experience and design accessibility and internationalization into the app from the start.
- **Open source**: Have an established practice of giving back to the open-source projects they use, including making upstream fixes and releasing internally developed tools and libraries.
- **Friendly to blogging**: Offer opportunities to write blog posts on interesting issues and engineering problems to share with the community, as well as sharing fun challenges and innovative solutions.
- **Sustainable**: Have a plan to be net zero. Potentially, be a registered B-corp (https://www.delawareinc.com/blog/what-is-a-certified-b-corporation/).
- **Flexible**: I didn't want to get stuck in a rigid 9-to-5!
- **Fun**: Doesn't take life too seriously. Personable and fun in documentation and onboarding, both internally and publicly.

Some of these may resonate with you, others may not be important at all. But coming up with a list that's personal to you makes it easier to work out what roles to apply for.

If you're not sure what aspects are important to you, discuss it with your family and friends. A different perspective is always useful.

Deciding on a Company Type

Once you've decided on the type of role you want to apply for and the culture you want to work in, it's time to narrow down the list of companies you want to work for by evaluating which company types are most likely to fit the bill. There are almost as many types of companies as there are roles in tech.

Working for a large company feels very different from a small company for their employees. Large companies tend to be more stable and usually have a well-defined career progression through the many roles within that company. When working at a large company, you have the opportunity to become an expert in a very narrow field. There's also more opportunity to work on projects that have a wider reach. Generally, you'll encounter more structure and clearer management at large companies, as well as well-defined communication workflows and documentation and processes. This may or may not suit you!

Smaller companies are very different. Start-ups are fast-moving and can be exciting and dynamic. You'll have more of an opportunity to make an impact and work on a wide range of problems. You'll also be required to help out in many functions that aren't necessarily part of your traditional role. As a software developer at a start-up, your day-to-day work will vary and you'll move between writing code, deploying apps, testing and being on-call to handle live issues. You might even be called to help out with marketing or customer service. In a large company, different people handle all these separate roles.

The common expectation is that start-ups offer better pay, whereas larger companies offer better stock options or benefits like pension plans and healthcare. A word of caution however — start-ups can be risky, especially if they haven't launched yet. Future companies want to see what you've worked on, and if the start-up fails before your app even reaches the App Store, it's difficult to showcase your work.

The size of a company influences its culture, but doesn't dictate it. Software developers are in high demand, so many companies, large and small, offer similar benefits, holidays and parental leave. Remember to think about what you want from a company, no matter its size.

Most people tend to gravitate to one company size over the other. Some people really enjoy working in a fast-paced environment that's constantly changing and getting to work in different types of roles. Others prefer the stability of a large company and the ability to focus on one thing, as well as not worrying whether the company will still exist next month!

Investigating the Company Culture

So, how do you know which companies are a good culture fit? You can start by looking for the company's core values. Usually found on their website, the core values tell you what a company thinks is important in terms of how it treats its customers and employees.

But how do you know whether a company really upholds its core values?

One of the best ways of getting an insight into a company is to look at their **engineering blogs**. Not only do these describe the kind of work you'll do, but they also give you a sense of the company's culture. You can see how much they invest in staff training, whether they use modern best practices for software development and how they work as a team. This can help you focus on companies that fit your personal criteria.

A comprehensive list of engineering blogs can be found at Kilimchoi's GitHub (https://github.com/kilimchoi/engineering-blogs). You can also follow employees on Twitter or LinkedIn to get an idea of what it's like to work for their company.

Remember, the interview is a great place to ask questions directly to company employees to find out about their culture.

Key Takeaways

- Before you start interviewing, determine the role and company type that are best for you.
- There are many different kinds of software engineers. There are also roles in tech beyond software engineering, like quality review, developer relations, security and data analysis.
- You should also consider the company size and aspects of the culture that matter most to you.
- Aside from salary, evaluate the perks and benefits a company offers.
- Doing solid research on a company before you apply will save you time and effort.

Resources

As you consider different software engineering roles and where you might want to work, here are some references to keep current on salary and working conditions:

- Stack Overflow's Annual Developer Survey (https://survey.stackoverflow.co/2022/) includes responses from more than 70,000 developers worldwide across many different tech stacks. In addition to seeing salary by developer type (https://survey.stackoverflow.co/2022/#work-salary) and all the different developer roles (https://survey.stackoverflow.co/2022/#developer-profile-developer-roles) represented in this survey, there's interesting data about top technologies, languages and more. You can also download the data set to do your own analysis.
- Kodeco's new State of Mobile Jobs (https://www.kodeco.com/state-of-mobile-jobs-2022) survey includes 1,257 responses from mobile developers around the world. You can set filters to explore salary by country or by programming language as well as a number of other factors, including benefits offered and developer educational background.
- Equity 101 for Software Engineers at Big Tech and Startups (https://blog.pragmaticengineer.com/equity-for-software-engineers/) offers a detailed discussion of how to evaluate equity, like stock or options, offered as part of a compensation package.

Action Plan

This chapter has given you a lot of things to think about before applying for your first role. Now, you should:

- Come up with a **list of non-negotiable requirements** for your desired job.
- Write down a **list of things that are nice to have** but you'd be willing to compromise on.
- Write a **pros and cons list** of working for a big or a small company, and decide which to target.
- **Identify five companies** that sound exciting to apply to. Investigate their culture by reading their engineering blogs and website.
- **Reach out to your network**, both in person and through LinkedIn or Twitter, to find people who work for those companies.

Reflect on what you've learned: Find this chapter's worksheet (PDF (https://github.com/kodecocodes/booh-materials/blob/editions/1.0/02-types-of-jobs-availableChapter02Worksheet.pdf)) in this book's GitHub materials repo.

Chapter 3: Decoding Job Listings to Find the Right Roles

By Tim Condon

When you start looking at job postings, you'll see a variety of different mobile dev titles and roles. For someone new to the industry, this can feel a little overwhelming. This chapter will show you how to navigate the complex market as you start looking for your first job in tech. By the end, you'll be able to decode job listings and discover the right job and level to apply for.

> **Note**: There's no industry standard for job roles, grades and titles — which also vary from country to country and company to company. This chapter tries to ensure that you can find the right roles to apply for, even when the titles vary dramatically.

What You'll Learn

This chapter will help you navigate confusing job listings so you can target the right roles for your skill set. Throughout the chapter, you'll learn:

- What different software engineering job titles mean.
- How to pick the right role and level to apply for.
- Real-world examples from job listings.
- How to set a general course for your future career.

You'll start with a deep dive into the tech titles you'll see in job postings and what they mean.

Exploring Tech Job Titles

Job titles are used primarily for distinguishing a role's level and area of expertise. A single company might have software engineering roles at a number of different levels, like so:

- Junior Software Engineer
- Software Engineer
- Senior Software Engineer
- Principal Software Engineer
- Staff Software Engineer
- And even more roles

> **Note**: In some countries, "engineer" is a protected job title, and you need specific qualifications to use it. This isn't common in the tech industry, so this book uses **engineer** and **developer** interchangeably.

As a recent graduate, you'll be most interested in the first two titles. However, it's never too early to start thinking about your future career path, so you'll take a brief look at the more senior titles as well.

Note that all of the experience requirements in this chapter are general estimates; realistically, the exact amount will vary depending on the companies you work for.

Junior Software Engineer (0 Years of Experience)

Junior software engineer or junior developer is the entry-level position in tech. Companies expect junior developers to have very little experience, if any. If you have only completed a short bootcamp or course of study, this is a good level to target.

Although junior software engineers are expected to have a strong foundation in their chosen programming language, they won't need to solve complex problems on their own. Instead, they work on basic implementations or pair with a more experienced developer to stretch their skills. They're expected to ask a lot of questions.

Necessary skills for this role include:

- A strong, demonstrated desire to learn and grow.
- Good communication skills including the ability to ask questions appropriately and listen and learn from colleagues.
- The ability to work well on a team.
- A strong foundation in the programming language(s) you were hired to use. Sometimes, even having taken advanced classes is enough to fulfill this requirement.

Many companies provide training at this level. The opportunity to attend seminars, conferences and other learning events is an important perk to ask about in the interview process.

Software Engineer (1–2 Years of Experience)

This is the place most people start their career in tech. If you've graduated from a computer sciences program or a longer course of study, or if you're confident in your general technical skills, you can apply for jobs at this level after graduation.

In this role, you'll be expected to know the basics of building apps for your chosen field — like a simple mobile app — and be able to explain some common basic programming concepts. You'll be expected to work in a team and help build apps with assistance and direction from senior developers.

Necessary skills for this role include:

- Experience writing software as part of full-time work, college/bootcamp coursework, personal projects, internships, coding competitions or research.
- Strong problem-solving skills and a passion for research and experimentation.
- Good teamwork and communication skills.
- A strong, demonstrated desire to learn and grow.

Additional skills that are helpful for this role:

- Exposure to architectural patterns.
- A basic understanding of testing and debugging.
- Exposure to CI/CD tools.

You won't be expected to make key decisions, decide on technical solutions or lead teams at this level.

Senior Software Engineer (5 Years of Experience)

After a few years of experience — somewhere around five years, though the exact time will depend on a mixture of your skill and how your company differentiates between levels — you'll progress to a **senior developer**. This role brings more responsibilities.

As a senior software engineer, you'll be expected to solve most problems without needing any help. When issues arise in your code, you'll be expected to debug and solve them. You should have a solid understanding of the platform you develop on.

At this level, you'll almost certainly be working closely with more junior team members, and you might be expected to mentor them. To this end, you need to be able to articulate solutions and explain problems in easy-to-understand ways.

Principal Software Engineer (7–8 Years of Experience)

When you reach principal, you'll usually look after a team of developers. At this level, you'll be able to find solutions for most problems you'll face. You'll have significant input into code development and architecture, and you'll be expected to know and ensure best practices are followed. You might be responsible for significant portions of an app — or even the whole thing.

If you work at a company with clients, you'll be expected to meet with them, demonstrate your apps and discuss — and implement — their feedback.

Staff Software Engineer and Above (10+ Years of Experience)

After around 10 years of experience, depending on your company, you'll need to decide whether to remain an individual contributor (IC) or go down the engineering manager role path. If you choose to stay on as an IC, a **staff engineer** role is a good position to target.

As a staff engineer, you'll be a specialist in your area of expertise. Expect to field questions that touch on your specialization from all over the company.

From here, you can continue to improve your skills and your specializations. You might move into a principal or distinguished software engineer role, or you might consider joining the management track as a Chief Technology Officer or other role. You'll eventually help guide the company in making technical decisions, such as when to adopt new technology.

Now that you have a good idea of the available roles as an IC, it's time to take a look at job descriptions to see which ones are a good fit for you.

Determining Which Level to Target

If you're applying for your first role in tech after graduating — either from a bootcamp, a computer sciences course or individual study — you'll probably apply at the base software engineer level. This is where most people who have a good software foundation but no professional experience will apply.

If you've only done a short bootcamp, or you've just started to study, you might target a junior level instead. As explained earlier, this also depends on the company and how it defines its levels.

This table gives you a basic idea of what skills are expected at the junior developer, software developer and senior software developer levels:

Skill	Level
Write and debug code	Junior software developer
Talk through solutions in code	Junior software developer
Improve skills and learn how to use new APIs and frameworks	Junior software developer
Independently implement features	Software developer
Review others' code	Software developer
Write unit tests for code to ensure code quality	Software developer
Mentor other team members	Senior software developer
Choose project architecture	Senior software developer
Explain technical problems in layman's terms to management and clients	Senior software developer

Skill expectations grow as you go up the levels.

Keep in mind that different companies expect different things from the roles they post. More important than a title is the demands the company lists for their roles. Reading through the job specification is the best place to start to work out what level to apply at. Next, you'll look at how to read job descriptions to determine whether they're right for you.

Deciphering Job Descriptions

When looking for roles to apply to, job descriptions can be a confusing mess of buzzwords! Sometimes, the perfect role might be masquerading under an unfamiliar title. So, you'll need to go beyond scanning job titles and read the job listings to work out whether a position is a good fit for your skills.

There are two main sections of the job description to look at: Qualifications and Responsibilities.

The **Qualifications** section provides a guideline for the experience you need to apply for the role. If a role only asks for educational experience, like a degree or bootcamp, then you probably qualify for it. If it requires multiple years of experience working on a platform, then you might want to put that on your "return to this in the future" list.

The **Responsibilities** section lists the key tasks you'll do day to day. Generally, if it lists points like "problem-solving" and "good understanding" of technical areas, then you should add it to the list to consider. If it lists points like "guiding other team members", "being a domain expert" or "independent problem-solving", then the description is probably aimed at more senior developers.

Now that you know what the job posting wants, the question is: Do you have what it takes?

Do You Have the Skills?

What happens if you look over a job posting that seems to be targeting your level but you feel like you don't have the skills you'll need?

Well, you might have much more applicable experience than you realize. Not all of the work requirements have to be done on the job; some can come from your bootcamp projects or classwork.

Go through all the projects you've done, skills you've learned and code you've written to build your listed qualifications. Working on a group project in a bootcamp is a great example. You worked as part of a team, communicated with teammates, defined clear requirements, built apps and ensured that your code worked cohesively. A single project hits many requirements listed for entry-level job descriptions!

Furthermore, not all of the experience has to be in a tech-related job. If you've worked in other industries or taken part-time jobs while studying, you can use those skills to enhance your resume. For example, any customer-facing role, like retail work, proves you can work as part of a team and with clients.

When you start looking for your first job, it's a good idea to look for ways to showcase your skills. Developing a portfolio is discussed more in Chapter 4, "Creating a Resume & Portfolio". Working on projects where others can see your code, which enhances your resume, is discussed in Chapter 8, "Building in Public".

> **Note**: For some tips on applying skills from non-technical experience to your resume, see Jay Strawn's article, How to Write the Perfect Resume After Graduating a Coding Bootcamp (https://www.kodeco.com/36875585-how-to-write-the-perfect-resume-after-graduating-a-coding-bootcamp).

Finally, it's worth applying to any roles that you find interesting or want to work at, even when you don't hit all the requirements — especially if the role is with a smaller, more flexible company. If the company likes you, they may try to fit you in even if you don't match the job description perfectly.

Next, you'll get some examples of real job postings that you can compare to your current skill set.

Examples of Real Job Posts

To look at a real-world example, here's a job description for a large tech company:

> **Key Job Responsibilities**
>
> • Design, develop and maintain our iOS mobile apps.
>
> • Work with team members to investigate design approaches, prototype technology and evaluate technical feasibility.
>
> • Lead architecture and design of features from conception to launch.
>
> • Help improve engineering processes and tools to increase team effectiveness.
>
> • Be part of an Agile development process to deliver high-quality software.
>
> **Basic Qualifications**
>
> • Experience contributing to the architecture and design (architecture, design patterns, reliability and scaling) of new and current systems.
>
> • Non-internship professional software development experience.
>
> • Programming experience with at least one modern language such as Java, C++ or C# including object-oriented design.

- Bachelor's degree in Computer Science, Computer Engineering or related field, or equivalent practical experience.
- Proficiency in Computer Science fundamentals such as object-oriented design, data structures, algorithm design, problem-solving and complexity analysis.
- iOS mobile application development experience in Objective-C and Swift.
- Experience communicating technical problems to both technical and business audiences verbally and in writing.

Preferred Qualifications

- Master's degree in Computer Science, Computer Engineering or related field or equivalent practical experience.
- Deep understanding of Agile principles and exposure to various process implementations.
- Proficient understanding of code versioning tools such as Git.
- Experience with reactive programming frameworks.
- Experience optimizing apps for performance.
- Experience writing testable code and automated tests.
- Experience with deployments to the App Store.
- Experience with REST architecture for web services.
- Knowledge of professional software engineering practices and best practices for full software development lifecycle, including coding standards, code reviews, source control management, continuous deployments, testing and operations.

In this example, the job posting is split into three sections: responsibilities, basic qualifications and preferred qualifications. The responsibilities section describes your day-to-day responsibilities. So, in this example, you'll work on iOS apps as part of a team. You might be responsible for building specific features, and you'll be expected to explain code and decisions to your team. The basic qualifications section shows what experience you should have.

When tailoring your resume for the job (See Chapter 4, "Creating a Resume & Portfolio"), you should ensure you have something for each point. So, in the above example:

- **Experience contributing to architecture and design**: You can use any complex app you've built as an example.
- **Professional software experience**: This may feel like it's excluding those who don't have any professional experience, but you may find this on graduate-level jobs. In most cases, you can use *any* work experience or projects for this, so don't let it put you off!
- **Experience with one modern language**: Everyone graduating from a bootcamp or computer science degree should have this!
- **Degree or equivalent experience**: Again, a bootcamp would also count for this.
- **Proficiency in computer science fundamentals**: You should cover some basics on this in your bootcamp or degree. This is also a pointer for things to look into when preparing for an interview.
- **iOS mobile app experience**: You should have this if applying for an iOS developer job! Going through some tutorials should suffice if it wasn't covered in your bootcamp or degree.
- **Experience communicating**: Any team projects you've done will count for this!

Overall, this posting is aimed at the software developer level, and most recent graduates with iOS development experience — either outside or during their education — would be fine applying.

The next example, for a clean energy company, is more clear-cut:

> **About you...**
>
> • You're someone who thrives on uncertainty and loves to make an impact.
>
> • You're passionate about what you do, and that shows through your enthusiasm and communication.
>
> • Your values align with the company's; you care about sustainability and creating a better future for our planet.
>
> • You enjoy contributing across the whole development process including design, product management and staying on top of upcoming technologies that could benefit the business.

What you'll have

• A computer science degree or equivalent (not essential but desirable).

• Can demonstrate having built one Android app as a hobby or as part of a degree.

• Knowledge and experience with Kotlin.

• Are keen to develop features across Android & iOS (previous exposure to iOS development is a plus, but not required).

• Are excited to learn new technologies like Jetpack Compose and GraphQL.

• Passionate about great app design and user experience.

The format of this posting is different, but the "About you" section provides some guidance about the type of company and its culture. The call-out to sustainability is easy to spot for someone who wants to work in an environmentally conscious company.

The "What you'll have" section provides the basic experience and qualifications you need. You can see that anyone who's done some Kotlin and built any kind of Android app would be able to apply. This job is aimed at junior developers and above.

The final example shows the other end of the spectrum:

Qualities and skills sought

• Solid industry experience building well-implemented and really usable native iOS and/or Android apps.

• A willingness to work dual-platform and across all aspects of the apps — you may cross-train within this role.

• Adept with Swift and/or Kotlin.

• Experience with SwiftUI and/or Jetpack Compose.

• Experience using SaaS APIs in a mobile app.

• Excellent analytical and problem-solving skills.

• Familiarity with best practice mobile app architectures.

• Familiarity with mobile unit testing.

• A self-starting, innovative and collaboration-oriented approach.

You can extract key details from this description. They expect experience in a number of areas you likely won't have covered in much depth, such as unit testing, architecture and working with different APIs. The first point for "solid industry experience" shows that they're looking for someone who's worked on a large professional app. Overall, this is aimed at the top end of software developers or senior software developers, so unlikely to be suitable to recent university or bootcamp graduates.

Remember that every company is different and that titles for equivalent roles vary, sometimes even from department to department within the same company! Read the job description thoroughly, and when in doubt, if you like the job, then apply. See Chapter 1, "Evaluating Your Options", for more on when to apply for different roles.

Thinking About Your Future

You're at an early stage in your career now, but as you gain experience, you'll also have more opportunities for advancement. Here's a quick look at how to interpret job levels and opportunities for promotion moving forward.

Interpreting Grades Within a Role

Some companies have different levels of seniority within each role. These levels, or grades, will determine your compensation. You'll move through the grades as you get more experience and take on more responsibilities.

When you first start out, target grade one. For example, "Software Engineer I" sounds like a good role to explore.

Getting Promoted

It's never too early to start thinking about your next steps, even as you're taking your first ones. One thing that you should consider as you start interviewing is your path to promotion once you get hired.

Most companies have specific processes for getting promotions. Some will require you to make your case to a promotion board, but this practice is becoming less common. Normally, when you start taking on responsibility and fulfilling the requirements of the grade above you, you or your manager will put you forward for promotion.

Many companies have a framework for determining what you need to do to progress in your career. For example, Monzo, a UK fintech company, has published its career progression framework (https://monzo.com/documents/engineering-progression-framework-v2-0.pdf). This describes the impact, technical skills and behaviors expected of you at each grade and level.

It's worth searching the website of the company you're applying to in case they publish a similar public framework.

Congratulations, you've made it to the end of the chapter! By this point in the book, you've learned which skills you need to apply, how to pick the kinds of companies you want to work for, and what the different job roles mean. Next, you'll look at how to create a resume and portfolio that will help you land an interview. Then you'll be ready to apply.

Key Takeaways

- Most people will apply for roles at the graduate level: Software Developer, Software Engineer or Junior Developer.
- Companies use different job descriptions for the same levels. Read the Qualifications section of a job listing to work out which roles are right for you.
- Don't be afraid to apply for roles that seem out of reach.

Action Plan

- **Write down your skills** from your bootcamp, experience and/or degree.
- Write down any potentially **relevant experience from other jobs**, even if they weren't in tech.
- Find job descriptions and **highlight key responsibilities and expectations**.
- Work out the **roles to apply for**.
- Pick out key responsibilities and qualifications from job descriptions and **match your skills** to them.

Reflect on what you've learned: Find this chapter's worksheet (PDF (https://github.com/kodecocodes/booh-materials/blob/editions/1.0/03-decoding-job-listings-to-find-the-right-roles/Chapter03Worksheet.pdf)) in this book's GitHub materials repo.

Chapter 4: Creating a Resume & Portfolio

By Tim Condon

Your resume or CV is the most important document you'll create during your job search. It summarizes your experience, knowledge and skills for companies so they know why they should hire you. This chapter will help you write a resume that's clear and helps you stand out from everyone else applying for the same roles.

What You'll Learn

This chapter covers different areas to consider when putting together your resume to send to prospective employers. You'll learn:

- What you should (and shouldn't!) include in a resume.
- How to tailor resumes to specific jobs.
- How automated applicant tracking systems (ATSs) work and how you can get past them.
- How to build a great portfolio.
- How and why to craft a great cover letter for each application.

By the time you're done, you'll be able to pair your completed resume with the jobs you discovered in the previous chapter to start your application process!

What to Include in Your Resume

Knowing what to include in your resume is hard, especially when you're applying for your first role in tech. After all, you don't have the luxury of professional experience in the tech industry yet. However, you can overcome this by using good examples from your education, previous non-technical jobs and other areas.

Remember, everyone applying for the same roles will be in the same position. Creating a compelling resume will help you stand out from other applicants.

Your resume should summarize your professional and other relevant experience and should be no longer than two pages. There's no single required format, but it should look professional.

> **Tip**: You can find a variety of professional resume templates (https://www.canva.com/resumes/templates/) for free at Canva.

You should ensure that the information is easy to scan and to read. Make sure your font is easy to read, the text is large enough and that there's ample white space so the page doesn't feel overcrowded. Use headings and bullet points appropriately.

Remember that the person reading the resumes might be viewing dozens or even hundreds of candidates; make it easy for them to see at a glance that you're a good candidate.

It's a good idea to tailor the design of your resume to the industry you're applying for. If you're applying for roles in a traditional industry, your resume design should be more conservative. If you're applying for a design company or a design role, you can have a bit more fun! But in all cases, it should be easy to scan, easy to read and smart. Avoid distracting colors or graphics.

Break your resume down into four distinct areas:

- Header
- Experience
- Education
- Skills

Next, you'll look at building each of these sections.

Creating Your Resume's Header

Your resume **header** sits at the top of the page and should have your name in the center in a large font. Below your name, include contact information — like your address, phone number and email address. If you have a website or GitHub profile, add it. Your custom LinkedIn URL (https://www.linkedin.com/help/linkedin/answer/a542685/manage-your-public-profile-url) also goes in this section.

Finally, add a short introduction about yourself in the header. The introduction should be a sentence or two that hooks the resume's readers so they look at your resume more closely. For example:

> Alice is a software developer with a passion for building well-designed and accessible iOS apps. She has a degree in history; she recently completed a coding bootcamp to pursue her passion for mobile development, where she built and shipped a music player app.

This showcases some of your drives (design and accessibility), gives a very brief overview of your experience and a real example of something you've built.

Including Your Education

Traditionally, the top section of the resume after the header and introduction is the experience section. However, if you've just completed your degree, you might not have any work experience to add.

When creating a resume for your first job in tech, your **education section** is most relevant to your job search, so you should put it before your experience.

Your education showcases what you've learned thus far. Add each education block in reverse chronological order with the most recent educational experiences listed first. What to include depends on your experience, age and what path you've taken in education.

If you have a university degree in computer science, then that should be the largest part of the education section. If you have a degree in an unrelated field, definitely include it, but without as much detail, as you'll add more information for a bootcamp or professional experience. You should also include your high school, but you only need to list the subjects you took and your grades. If you don't have a degree, then you can include your high school and expand more on either the bootcamp you've done or any relevant professional experience.

Your tech degree or bootcamp should provide a high-level overview of all the topics you've learned. List the specific technologies and areas you studied. Be sure to provide success stories from projects you worked on. When using group projects, be clear about your responsibilities and which parts you worked on. For example:

> Built an e-commerce site for our final group project in the bootcamp. I was responsible for building an API to handle orders and process payments. I worked closely with the web developer to ensure that requests from the website to the API worked correctly and provided what they needed. The project took three weeks and worked successfully. The API was built using NodeJS; orders were saved in PostgreSQL.

This provides a clear overview of the project and what you directly worked on. It showcases your teamwork as you worked with other developers, experience building a complex system and the technologies you used. These are all things that employers will look for when reading resumes.

Adding Your Experience to Your Resume

Even if you've never worked a tech job, you still need an **experience section**. If you've had any previous jobs, even part-time while in college, you'll list them here. Of course, if you've had any previous experience in tech jobs or internships, you should definitely include them!

For each job, add your title, place of work and dates in reverse chronological order, with the most recent first. Then, for each job, add a few bullet points highlighting your achievements in the role. Don't be afraid to take credit for the work you did, even when working as a team. For example, if you worked in a restaurant, you could say:

> Worked as a server responsible for ensuring 30 tables were looked after and happy. Handled complaints to the kitchen and ensured they were all resolved.

This shows you worked in a high-pressure environment, interacting with lots of different customers and managing any issues. All these skills are relevant, even in tech. Any experience you've gained in *any* role is applicable. Some skills that companies want to see and things you'll use in a tech job include:

- Learning to work as a team.
- Communicating well with customers, managers and other team members.
- Writing and organizational skills.
- Problem-solving abilities.
- Leading teams and organizing camps.

If you do have experience in tech, either working on your own side projects or doing an internship, you should be clear about what you achieved and the technologies you worked on.

For example, if you did a two-month internship working on mobile apps, you could say:

> • Spent two months working on an internal iOS app as part of a team of three. I was responsible for the inventory page, ensuring that the service desk could add, track and remove company assets.
>
> • Used Swift and SwiftUI to build the app.
>
> • Helped automate builds to the enterprise App Store to ensure that changes were released more quickly. I wrote the scripts for CI to automatically build any code changes.

This provides some insight into the work you did and what you already know. You'll likely be asked about these points in your interview, as they provide interesting discussion topics, so only use what you worked on yourself.

In the example above, even if you're applying for a role that doesn't include working on iOS apps, you should still include all of the information about your past experience. Many skills transfer directly to other languages and other tech roles.

Listing Your Skills on Your Resume

The final section on your resume should be a **skills section** that provides an easy list to look at to see if you match the role. Think of this section as a keyword list that will be used by recruiters, interviewers and automated applicant tracking systems.

You should add all the technologies you've worked with, including different programming languages, frameworks and design skills. If you're applying for roles in a different language than your native tongue, you should also include your language skills.

Finishing Up

Once you've put your resume together, it's a good idea to get someone else to look over it. This can be a friend, a recruiter you're working with, someone in tech or — even better — a mentor. They can look over it to make sure it makes sense and is readable. They'll be able to give you advice on any parts that need to be expanded or rewritten. For example, any sections that don't explain what you specifically did in a group project should be changed to be more explicit about your contributions.

You should also have someone else check each version of your resume when you tailor it for specific roles. You'll learn about this later in the chapter.

What Not to Include in Your Resume

While you should include as much relevant experience as you can in your resume, there are some things you *don't* want to include. Generally, you shouldn't include any education before the age of 16. And you don't need to include the award for best Halloween costume from preschool!

You might find that if you've had several jobs before changing to a career in tech, you'll struggle to fit everything onto two pages. If you're changing careers, it's a good idea to include all jobs you've had since school so you can explain what you've done in your professional career, but you don't need to include earlier jobs.

However, if you're applying to your first job straight out of university, then definitely include jobs from school and college, as you can use these to showcase your skills in communication and working in a team.

You also shouldn't include any images or diagrams, as these take up valuable space and won't do a good job of conveying your experience.

> **Note**: Resume dos and don'ts vary by region. For example, in the US, you don't want to include a photograph, whereas this is standard practice elsewhere. If you're applying for a job based outside your region, get a local to review your resume and ask, "Is there anything I've included that you would recommend removing?"

Tailoring Resumes

If you follow the steps from this chapter so far, you'll end up with a strong resume that you can hand out at job fairs or other recruiting events. However, if you're applying for individual roles, you should spend some time tailoring your resume to the specific job you're applying for.

For example, in a group project, you might've had multiple responsibilities working on the Android app and also the back end. If you apply to a back-end role, then your Android app work should be a single bullet point. However, you should go into detail about the work you did on the back end, the technologies you used and how you tied it all together. Alternatively, if you apply for an Android role, then the back-end work should be a bullet point, and you should go into detail about the UI frameworks you used to build the app, any networking libraries you used and so on.

In Chapter 3, "Decoding Job Listings to Find the Right Roles", you learned how to decipher job listings and discover the different skills the job might require. You can use this to determine which parts you need to emphasize and highlight in your resume.

> **Important**: A good rule of thumb is to go through the required skills in the job description and make sure you specifically mention as many of those as you have experience for in your resume. This will give you a much higher chance of being noticed compared to submitting a generic resume.

When I was applying for my first jobs, I created a base template that included the information I needed for every application, such as my pre-university education, grades and the summer job I worked for several years in a restaurant. I expanded this to emphasize how I had experience working in a team, juggling several different tasks and demonstrating good communication. As I studied computer science at university, I wrote only a few bullet points about the major topics covered, such as the languages I'd learned and the main modules I'd taken.

Then, when I applied for different roles, I expanded upon my university experience and my side project of building websites, where that information made sense. When I applied for a role building internal support systems for a company, I went into detail about the different sites I'd built and showcased my experience creating web apps. I also expanded on a group project where we had to gather requirements from a number of different groups in the university to build them an app to help promote student societies. This demonstrated my experience working with different groups to understand requirements — a listed required skill on the job ad.

Another job I applied for was working in cybersecurity. For this one, I changed my resume to expand upon the security and network modules I'd taken. The job ad asked for experience working in C and Assembly, so I wrote several bullet points on my final year project where I used these languages extensively.

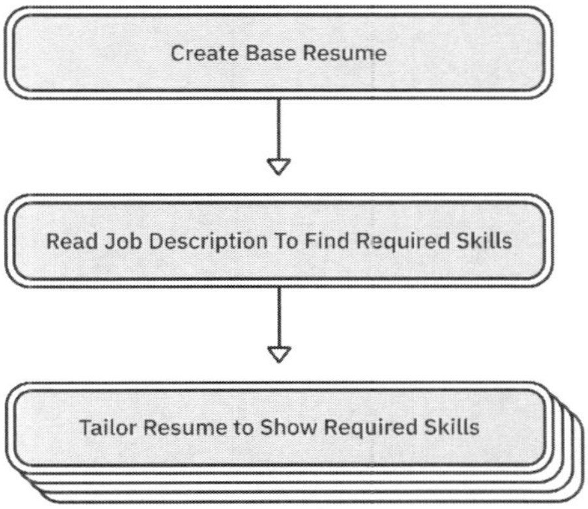

Start with a base resume, then craft a unique version for each position you seek.

Remember that some of the people screening your resume might not be technical themselves. Instead, they have a list of keywords to watch out for. By ensuring that your resume closely matches the requirements listed in the job posting, you increase your chances of progressing in the application process and securing that interview!

Managing Applicant Tracking Systems

Applicant tracking systems (or ATSs) are commonly used by large companies that need to track thousands of job applications for various different roles. They differ depending on the company, but usually ask you to answer some questions about your experience — e.g., "Tell me a time when you solved a difficult technical problem" — and to submit your resume. If you're lucky, you can submit your resume as a PDF or Word document, but be warned: Some systems require you to manually enter details into an online form.

ATSs commonly have a screening function where the system automatically rejects candidates that don't match the criteria for the role. Whenever you apply to a role that requires you to use an online system to track your application, make sure you read through the job description and use the same phrases and keywords it mentions. Don't be afraid to copy phrases such as "experience building web applications" word for word in your application.

The skills section of your resume is another good place to list the exact skills you have that the application is looking for. Doing this ensures you have the highest possible chance of getting through the automated screening and continuing to the next stage.

> **Tip**: If you need to answer long-form questions on the sites, write your answers in a local document and save it. Not only does this save you time if the system crashes when you try to submit your answers, but you may also find that different companies use the same underlying ATS and have the same questions, saving you time in your job search!

Building a Portfolio

A **portfolio** is your chance to show off projects you've worked on. This is a great opportunity to stand out from other prospective developers when none of you are likely to have real work experience in tech.

If you're applying for most developer roles, then you can quickly build a portfolio using a **GitHub** profile. GitHub is a popular website for hosting source code; if you've gone through any online tutorials or courses, it's a good idea to make the code you've written public there. Don't worry about making the code perfect — no one expects that.

Your profile allows employers to see contributions, discussions on pull requests and issues and the different projects you've worked on. This can also make for great topics to discuss in an interview. For more details on projects to include on GitHub, check out Chapter 8, "Building in Public" and Chapter 9, "Learn & Share".

Your GitHub profile should have pinned repositories showing your best apps or projects that you've contributed to. If you're part of any organizations, then you can make these public as well.

Finally, create a GitHub Profile README (https://docs.github.com/en/account-and-profile/setting-up-and-managing-your-github-profile/customizing-your-profile/managing-your-profile-readme). This gives you a space to introduce yourself and describe what kinds of things you enjoy building.

For example, here's my GitHub profile:

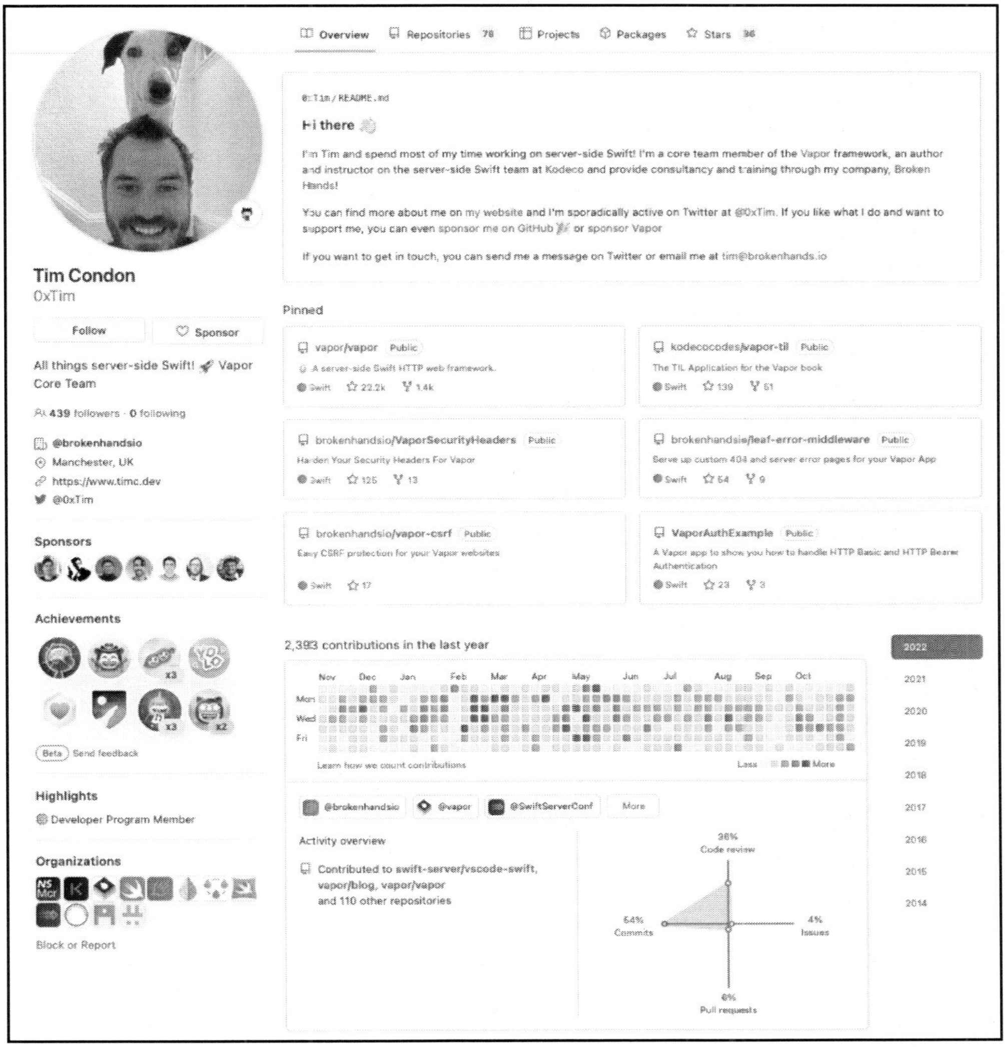

Take the time to design a GitHub profile that showcases your work.

This took little effort to make, and it provides a good place to point people to. It gives me a quick introduction, shows some of the projects I've worked on and showcases my contributions.

For most developers, this will be more than good enough. However, if you're applying to do website development or any kind of design work, you should build a real portfolio website. This should include any projects you've worked on and examples of your work.

You can even use your portfolio to display example sites that aren't real. If I'm looking to hire a designer or web developer, I won't consider them if they don't have their own site showing what they can do.

Your portfolio *must* look good! After all, you can't expect anyone to employ you to build great-looking websites if you can't build one for yourself. So, spend a bit of time building a simple portfolio and a couple of example sites, if necessary. You should also add links to your GitHub account, any blogs you've written and ways to contact you.

Crafting a Cover Letter

When applying to a job, you should always send a cover letter along with your resume. The only exception to this is when you apply via an ATS and submit everything through the service.

If you're applying via email, then the email is your cover letter; otherwise, you should write a separate letter.

Use your cover letter to introduce yourself to whoever reads your application. Explain why you're interested in the job and what you offer to the role.

It needs to make a good first impression, because if it doesn't, they may not even read your resume. The cover letter only needs to be a few paragraphs — in fact, any longer may put people off! If they have to go through a hundred applications, they won't want to read several pages of a cover letter.

Your cover letter should be split into two sections. The first section should cover why you want to apply for the job. Go into detail about what appeals to you about the role or the company. It could be the chance to work for a company that built an app you use every day, or it might be that the role uses a specific web framework you've been using and working with. You *must* personalize this section and make it specific to the role and company you're applying to.

Generic cover letters are extremely easy to spot, and they don't create a good impression — you'll likely be rejected in favor of someone who's explained why they want the role.

The second section should cover what you offer to the role. Pick one or two of the required skills that you satisfy and explain why you'd be great in the role. Selling yourself can be hard to do, but if you persuade the person reading your application that you're a great fit, you'll encourage them to read your resume and advance you to the next stage of the process.

Finally, make sure the cover letter doesn't have any spelling mistakes or grammatical errors in it. Use a website like Grammarly (https://app.grammarly.com/) to provide a first pass. Then, ask someone else to proofread it to make sure it's all correct.

An example of a bad cover letter is:

> To who it may concern,
>
> I'm Tim and have just finished my university corse in computer science. I'm interested in the mobile developer role I saw advertised for you company as I want do mobile development. I helped build a mobile app during my course and think I have the skills listed in the job ad. You can see my resume which I have attach to this email.
>
> Thanks,
>
> Tim

If I saw this cover letter with twenty other applications, I'd likely reject it without reading the resume for three major reasons:

1. It contains a number of spelling and grammatical errors, which gives the impression that the applicant didn't even take the time to ensure it's right — which won't make companies want that person to work for them.
2. It's generic and doesn't explain why they want to work for this company. It could be written for any mobile developer job.
3. Finally, it doesn't do a good job showcasing the applicant's skills and what they offer to the role.

Compare that cover letter to a good example:

> Hi Sarah,
>
> I'm Tim, and I'd love to have the opportunity to apply for the mobile developer role at Monzo. I've been a Monzo user for two years now and would relish the opportunity to work on an app I use every day! I've been following Monzo's engineering blog for a while and especially enjoyed the post discussing building a common design language for mobile apps.
>
> I've just graduated university with a 2.1 in computer science; as part of my course, I did several modules on mobile development. I believe I would be a strong addition to the team, as I have already built a few apps and I have a passion for creating great user experiences, just like the Monzo app does. I've attached my resume to the email, which provides more details about my experience.
>
> Thanks for considering my application,
>
> Tim

This is a much better letter; it's polite, has no spelling or grammar errors and offers a far more compelling case to consider the application. Several things in this cover letter make it stand out:

- If you're sending your application to a specific person, use their name. It makes the application much more personable.
- By mentioning the company you're applying to, what they work on and why you want to work for them, you sound much more enthusiastic.
- The point mentioning the blog clearly shows that this isn't a copy-and-paste letter and that you already have an interest in the company and app.
- This letter explains the skills you offer and sounds much more engaged.

Cover letters can be time-consuming and difficult to write, especially if you're applying to a company you've never heard of before. There's absolutely nothing wrong with applying for a role because it's just a job. However, by spending a bit of time researching the role and company, then using that research to personalize your cover letter, you have a much better chance of standing out.

Key Takeaways

- Keep the resume relevant and focused on your experiences in tech.
- Adapt every time you apply to maximize your chances of progressing through the application process.
- Relevant skills can come from any experience in education, previous jobs and hobbies — you don't need tech-specific experience for everything.
- A portfolio or GitHub account is very useful to showcase your skills and help you stand out from the crowd.
- Ask a mentor or friend to check your resume for errors and readability.

Resources

- How to Write a Resume as a Bootcamp Graduate (https://www.kodeco.com/36875585-how-to-write-a-resume-as-a-bootcamp-graduate) shows how to include personal projects and non-tech work experience so your skills shine through.
- How to Write a Killer Software Engineering Résumé (https://www.freecodecamp.org/news/writing-a-killer-software-engineering-resume-b11c91ef699d/) gives another perspective on how to write a resume for a software role.
- How to Write an ATS-Friendly Resume (https://www.myperfectresume.com/career-center/resumes/how-to/ats-friendly) explains how to write a resume that makes it past applicant tracking system screens by including keywords from job listings.
- These detailed packets from Harvard's Office of Career Services guide for undergraduate (https://hwpi.harvard.edu/files/ocs/files/undergrad_resumes_and_cover_letters.pdf) and graduate students (https://hwpi.harvard.edu/files/ocs/files/gsas-cvs-and-cover-letters.pdf) give advice about preparing resumes, cover letters and, for grad students, CVs.
- How to Create a Portfolio Website – A Beginner Developer's Guide (https://www.freecodecamp.org/news/beginners-guide-to-creating-a-portfolio-website/) is a brief introduction to what you should include when building a portfolio website.

Action Plan

- **Create a base resume** containing all the standard sections explained earlier in this chapter.
- **Tailor the resume to each role** by highlighting specific experience and technologies you used to match the job posting.
- **Create your GitHub account** and add a profile README. Start publishing your work to showcase it.
- **Build a portfolio website** to show off your design skills, if necessary.

Reflect on what you've learned: Find this chapter's worksheet (PDF (https://github.com/kodecocodes/booh-materials/blob/editions/1.0/04-creating-a-resume-and-portfolio/Chapter04Worksheet.pdf)) in this book's GitHub materials repo.

Chapter 5: Traditional & Nontraditional Ways to Find Jobs

By Jennifer Bailey

Now that you've created your resume and portfolio, the next step is to find great positions to apply to. There are a lot of different ways to find jobs, and having so many options might leave you feeling anxious or overwhelmed. Don't worry if you feel that way — this book is here to help. You're about to embark on a quest, and who knows what treasure you'll uncover along the way!

In this chapter, you'll cover where to start looking for jobs. It will include some tips on how to leverage job sites and other traditional methods, as well as some tips you might not have thought of yet.

What You'll Learn

- How to use hiring sites to look for jobs.
- Where and how to make connections that could lead to new opportunities.
- How to seek out opportunities that aren't on job boards.
- How to make the most of the resources you already have.

There's no time like the present to find some open roles that match your skills and apply!

Traditional Versus Nontraditional Ways to Find Jobs

Many people use traditional methods to find their perfect roles, and for good reason: they're tried and true because they're effective. These methods include:

- Using hiring websites.
- Attending career fairs and other events.
- Networking with developer communities.
- Creating connections with recruiters and employers.

Traditional methods are easy to use and sometimes give you important information about companies to apply to or how to improve your application. However, a lot of people use these methods, which means you'll have more competition.

That's why you'll also learn about nontraditional job search methods. Most people never consider creating their own opportunities. This chapter will show you how to do that — and how easy it can be!

You'll start by exploring the most common traditional job search tool: the hiring website.

Finding a Job Using Hiring Websites

Hiring websites are the most common place to find and apply for open positions. These websites are widely used by employers and applicants, and there are many to choose from.

Here are some popular options:

- LinkedIn Jobs (https://www.linkedin.com/jobs/): LinkedIn is the single most important tool you'll use in your job search. It's the top professional networking platform, which makes it a great way to find jobs across the globe. Best of all, it cuts down on the "noise" of so many available roles by tailoring the jobs you see to your skills and resume. The downsides to LinkedIn include needing a paid plan to access all the features and an interface that isn't the most intuitive.

- Indeed.com: Indeed is the largest job posting website, boasting over **3 million** jobs — and it's free for job seekers! It offers powerful features like email notifications that let you receive new job postings matching your search criteria. Indeed also includes company reviews and helpful articles and videos. It's straightforward to use, although you have to apply for each job individually. Indeed posts jobs worldwide. Some similar competitors to Indeed include ZipRecruiter (https://www.ziprecruiter.com/) and CareerBuilder (https://www.careerbuilder.com/).

- Women Who Code Job Board (https://www.womenwhocode.com/jobs): The Women Who Code job board has active postings from Women Who Code Partners that have made a commitment to hiring diverse candidates for a more equitable tech industry. There are roughly 200 active jobs at a time. You can search the board by experience level and whether an opportunity offers contract, part or full time work.

- Monster (https://www.monster.com/): Monster has been around since 1999, and it's still a leading platform that features jobs from around the world. It lets job seekers upload a resume and search for jobs at no cost, and its interface is easy to use. You can hide that you're looking for work from your current employer, if you have one.

- Dice (https://www.dice.com/): Dice is popular for tech-specific jobs. It's free and user-friendly for job seekers, and it includes a strong matching feature to find compatible companies. Dice offers an option to quickly apply for jobs, a mobile app and a salary estimator. Keep in mind, however, that it features only U.S. jobs.

- The Muse (https://www.themuse.com/): The Muse boasts 7 million monthly users, along with detailed company profiles and career coaching. One of the downsides to the site is that it's only available in English.
- Glassdoor (https://www.glassdoor.com/): Glassdoor really shines as a tool where you can get a feel for a company and its culture. You can see a company's size and age and read reviews from people who've worked there. Some employers even provide information about their interviewing process. It's not the clearest or easiest to use, but it does have great job filtering options.
- Tech Ladies (https://www.hiretechladies.com/): Tech Ladies is a woman-specific site that boasts a global community of 100,000 members. You need to apply for the site. After you're approved, you can access a free job board. You can also take advantage of live webinars on a variety of topics to support you in your career development.
- FlexJobs (https://www.flexjobs.com/): FlexJobs is highly rated for finding remote work around the world, although most of the jobs are based in the U.S. Use it to search for full-time, part-time or freelance remote positions. It offers career coaching, events and a wealth of articles, though you'll need a paid account to use all its features. The interface is a bit busy, but it's one of the best options for finding work-at-home positions.
- Eurojobs.com: Eurojobs.com is the largest job search site that posts opportunities from Europe. You can search by country and filter via job category. Using this job site is free, and it also includes many articles about working in Europe.

This list is only a sampling of popular job sites, but using them will help you find a wide variety of jobs that fit your criteria. If you need more job websites, Google is your friend. Also, if you're applying to large companies such as Google or Meta, they have their own hiring portals on their company sites. It's a good idea to check for job listings directly from the company's website.

Next, you'll learn what to consider when choosing a hiring website.

Selecting Hiring Websites

There are a lot of hiring websites, and you only have a limited amount of time each day to search, so it's important to narrow your options when selecting which ones to use.

Start by thinking about what's important to you in a job. Then you can pick hiring websites that focus on those aspects.

For example:

- Some specialize in certain countries or localized areas, while others provide a global job search. Are you willing to relocate?
- Some have more postings specific to remote work; others are better for a local search. Would you rather work from home or in an office setting?
- Some are tech-specific or even role-specific, whereas other sites cater to all industries. How flexible are you in the positions you're looking for?
- Some are more convenient than others and have fewer steps to apply — but you also have more competition. How much effort are you willing to put into dealing with each website?

It's a good idea to put your resume on many different sites to get it in front of as many different hiring agents as you can. Note which ones have the most promising positions and revisit them often.

Don't despair if the application process takes quite some time when you start. As you explore the job sites, you'll gain experience with the tools. Soon, you'll be making the most efficient use of your time and giving your resume the widest reach possible.

Consistency is an important part of your search. To keep from being overwhelmed, set aside a specific time each day to search through job listings, then commit to that time period. Don't let yourself avoid the task, but also don't allow yourself to overshoot the time you put aside for it.

Avoiding Scams

Unfortunately, job seekers can be targeted by scams. Many hiring sites verify their job listings to reduce spam, but some still gets through. Use your common sense, instincts and web safety protocol when utilizing job sites.

Below are some things that should put you on high alert:

- You were contacted by a company that you didn't reach out to first.
- The offer is too good to be true; for example, the salary is too high for what the position normally pays.

- You are offered a job without going through an interview process.
- The job description and requirements are vague.
- You notice a lot of errors or unprofessional writing in the correspondence.
- The company wants to interview you via a messaging service like WhatsApp, without any video or phone interviews included in the process.
- Contact information is unclear, invalid or not provided.
- You use the WHOIS database to look up the company and find the domain doesn't exist.
- The recruiter asks for confidential or financial information.
- You're asked to pay money for any reason.

This checklist includes just a few of the things to watch out for to avoid a scam job posting. Of course, not every one of the things listed are sure signs of scams. For example, if you post your resume on a hiring site, you hope people will reach out to you first. If this happens, however, take a few minutes to research the company that contacted you before responding.

On the other hand, some things are always a red flag. For example, there's never a good reason to pay someone for a job or to get an interview.

It's easy to react in the moment when on the hunt for a job. Be sure to think before you act and protect your private information.

Congratulations! You've learned a lot about job sites and how to explore the available resources, which has helped prepare you to find opportunities as they surface. Next, you'll learn about another traditional way of finding jobs: networking.

Networking

Another traditional way to find jobs is by building connections. According to a LinkedIn study (https://news.linkedin.com/2017/6/eighty-percent-of-professionals-consider-networking-important-to-career-success), 70% of people found jobs through their connections. In today's developer environment, there are lots of great ways to network, no matter where you live or what part of tech you find exciting.

Next, you'll learn about networking options including:

- Career fairs
- Events and conferences
- Clubs for developers
- Online communities and newsletters
- Networking with recruiters and employers

Attending Career Fairs

If you're a recent or soon-to-be college grad, you're most likely familiar with career fairs, where employers come to campus in search of entry-level hires. Definitely plan to attend any of these that include companies looking for software engineers.

You can find upcoming career fairs on your campus through your school's placement office, your Handshake (https://joinhandshake.com/students/how-it-works/) account or by searching your school's name plus "career fair" online.

If you've graduated from a software development bootcamp, the bootcamp might host its own career fair, most likely online. Ask them about networking opportunities and what other job placement assistance they can offer.

> **Tip**: Learn more about virtual career fairs, including where to find them and how to prepare, in U.S. News' article, What to Know About Virtual Career Fairs (https://money.usnews.com/money/blogs/outside-voices-careers/articles/what-to-know-about-virtual-career-fairs).

Attending Events

Attending events and conferences gives you different ways to discover open positions. For example, conferences are often sponsored by companies that are hiring, while it's common for recruiters to attend to meet candidates.

You can use tools like Meetup (https://meetup.com) to find events in your area. After you sign up, add your interests and search for engaging clubs and groups.

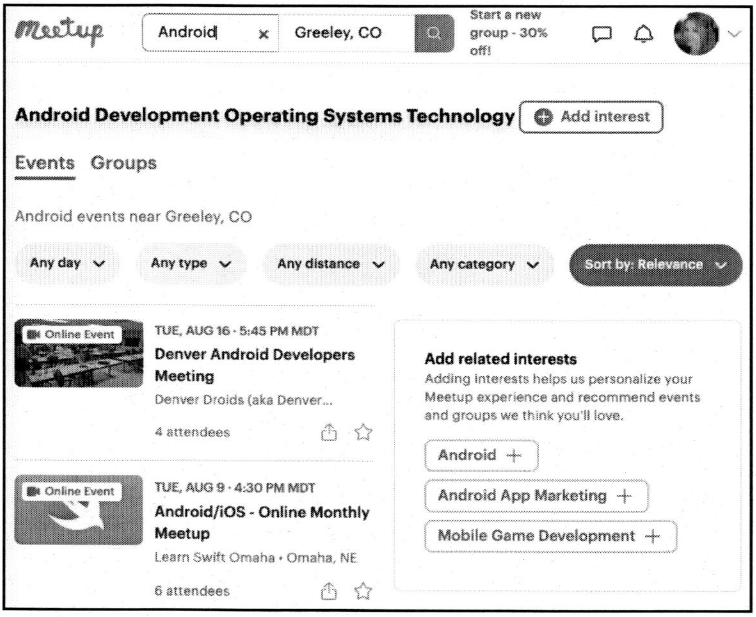

Meetup is a great place to find networking events.

Many popular events in the mobile app development sphere center around iOS and Android, but don't despair if you're a Flutter developer; more Flutter events are popping up as the framework gains popularity.

You can also use Google to find local events. Use search terms like "droid con", "Android events", "Android conferences" or "iOS events". Lists of developer events online are another helpful resource. Here are some examples:

- Cocoa Conferences (https://cocoaconferences.com/) lists conferences for iOS, macOS, watchOS and tvOS developers.
- Android Study Group (https://androidstudygroup.github.io/conferences/) has a list of upcoming Droidcons and other events for Android developers.

- Flutter.dev's site (https://flutter.dev/events) has a section for upcoming Flutter events.

Online events and conferences are useful and generally more affordable than their in-person counterparts. However, face-to-face contact is powerful. It's a good idea to look for both options.

> **Note**: For tips on making online conferences work for you, read Professional Networking at Virtual Conferences: How to Connect Online (https://www.kodeco.com/30863967-professional-networking-at-virtual-conferences-how-to-connect-online).

Getting the Most From Conferences You Attend

When you attend a conference, you'll learn a lot from the speakers, but as a job seeker, the people you meet will be just as important. Here are some ways to make conferences work for you.

Building Connections

Many conferences use Slack or Discord to help participants stay in touch. If you have this option, be sure to join and say hello in the channel to start building connections with other attendees.

It's tempting to hide out and just listen at a conference, but working the crowd gives you a much bigger advantage. Here are some things you can do:

- Strategically plan to attend the networking sessions and let people know that you're open to employment.
- If you see people who have a job similar to the one you'd like, strike up a conversation. Ask them for tips and advice.
- Ask the people you chat with what they think about their jobs and if their companies are hiring.

It can feel nerve-wracking to put yourself out there, but it just might lead you to your next position. And even if you don't immediately find job openings through your networking, you will meet some interesting people willing to help you on your career journey.

Making It Easy for People to Reach You

When you sign up for a conference, be sure to come prepared. If you meet someone who's interested in discussing a job with you, be sure to have your contact information handy, including links to your resume and social media profiles.

If you're attending in person, consider going the extra step and bring a printed resume or business cards. Be sure to include a link that lets people view your resume and connect with you more easily.

LinkedIn's app offers an easy way to do this: a QR code (https://www.linkedin.com/help/linkedin/answer/a525286/using-a-linkedin-qr-code-to-connect-with-members?lang=en) that links to your profile.

To create a custom QR code, tap the search bar:

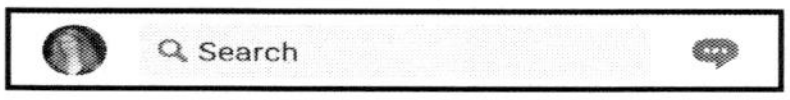

On the right, you'll see a **QR code** button:

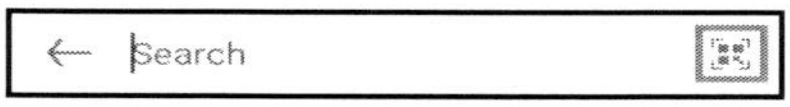

Tap that to generate a QR code that links to your profile.

There's also a **Scan** tab that will allow you to scan someone else's QR code:

This is a great way to quickly add contacts on the go.

Following up After the Conference

As you meet interesting people, be sure to follow them on social media and encourage them to follow you as well. This helps you keep in touch after the conference. Over time, this is how you build your network.

It's also a good idea to follow the presenters and speak to them if they're available after their sessions. Make a note of any promising connections you make, then follow up. Putting yourself out there isn't always comfortable, but you may discover new leads, contacts and even friends.

> **Challenge**: At your next conference, set a goal to introduce yourself to at least five new people and exchange contact information. If you're comfortable, you might be able to exceed this number. This is a great way to grow and move outside your comfort zone.

Participating in Clubs for Developers

Aside from conferences, there are other clubs and events that meet to discuss different technologies. Seeking out and joining these clubs can put you in touch with people working in areas that interest you.

A good place to find these clubs is Meetup.com. You can also check with your local city or county government, local schools and colleges and your local library or recreation center.

Here are some examples of popular clubs for developers:

- Google Developer Group (https://developers.google.com/community/gdg)
- Microsoft-sponsored developer communities (https://developer.microsoft.com/en-us/community/)
- iOS Dev Happy Hour (https://www.iosdevhappyhour.com/)

At these events, you have a good chance of running into people who are either seeking talent themselves or know someone who is. Meanwhile, you'll stay informed about what's new and exciting with your platform — which is also an advantage for your job search.

Next, you'll learn about other resources to find jobs, including online communities and email lists.

Joining Online Communities

Like job sites, there are a vast number of online communities and email lists. To find them, think of the technologies, platforms and code languages you're most interested in working with, then search for those terms. Adding "+newsletter" and "+community" to your search is helpful.

Reddit (https://www.reddit.com/) has communities centered around various technologies — and even job-specific communities. There, you can talk to people and ask questions.

Another good place to find developers is Medium (https://medium.com/). Use it to find out who's writing about interesting topics and connect with those people.

Searching for popular platforms and code languages will lead you to Slack and Discord channels devoted to them. It's a good idea to join these and check in periodically. Here, you can ask and answer questions and make connections with the people you meet.

Don't overlook newsletters like Android Weekly (https://androidweekly.net/). Even if those newsletters don't post jobs specifically, they help you stay informed of the latest news about your platform. Sometimes, email newsletters spotlight people, companies or events — and they might even hire tech writers themselves.

> **Tip**: Make a specific label or folder in your email for these mailing lists so that you can join as many as you like without filling your inbox.

Additionally, you can join organizations that concentrate on certain segments of the tech community. There are many groups for women, for example:

- Women Techmakers (https://developers.google.com/womentechmakers)
- Women Who Code (https://www.womenwhocode.com/)
- Lesbians Who Tech & Allies (https://lesbianswhotech.org/)

You could also look for groups that focus on any other segment of the population you identify with. An internet search will bring up many more opportunities.

Once you've found and joined some great online communities for your platform, you need to leverage them actively to build connections. Simply joining or subscribing is a good start, but you need to take additional steps like:

- Checking in periodically. Set a reminder so the communities you follow don't fall off your radar.
- Trying to be helpful. Answer as many questions as you can, even if it's only to point someone toward useful resources.
- Reaching out to people and building connections.
- Searching for leads about new jobs and new ways to put yourself out there.

> **Challenge**: Set a goal of reaching out to leads you've found in online communities to inquire about positions at least once per week.

By joining online communities and subscribing to interesting newsletters, you'll receive learning opportunities, mentorship and new ways to grow in your field. Next, it's time to connect with recruiters and employers.

Networking With Recruiters and Employers

As you search for jobs, you'll come across names of interesting companies and recruiters. When you do, be sure to capture these contacts for your network.

Many employers and recruiters have a presence online, so be sure to follow them on places like Twitter or LinkedIn. That will help you learn more about what they do and see if they're posting opportunities in their feed. Many recruiters offer tips for job searchers in their social media posts.

A good place to find recruiters is through agencies that specialize in tech recruiting. Searching for phrases like "tech recruiting agencies for mobile developers" or for your specific platform will give you some options. Learn more in Chapter 6, "Working With Recruiters".

As you find employers that interest you, research them further on sites like Glassdoor (https://www.glassdoor.com/index.htm) or on hiring websites. This will give you an idea if their corporate values align with your priorities and if other developers enjoy working there.

Nontraditional Ways to Find Jobs

You can take a deep breath and pat yourself on the back. At this point, you've learned how to use the most common traditional means of finding a job in tech. You'll now get creative and explore some of the nontraditional ways to find a job.

According to CNBC (https://www.cnbc.com/2019/12/27/how-to-get-a-job-often-comes-down-to-one-elite-personal-asset.html), up to 70% of jobs are not published.

So, how can you find jobs that employers don't publish? You can uncover opportunities in different ways. Technology is widespread across many industries worldwide, and everyone's life is affected by it — which means that tech jobs can turn up in unexpected places. Sometimes, people need your expertise and don't even know it yet.

In this section, you'll learn about:

- Finding tech roles in unexpected places.
- Reaching out directly to companies you'd love to work for.
- Creating opportunities.
- Using your existing connections.

These methods let you use your creativity to get an edge over other developers competing for a role.

Targeting Companies Outside the Industry

When you consider dev jobs, you might immediately think about working for a famous tech company like Microsoft, Google or Meta. However, every industry needs technology to thrive these days, and job seekers often overlook lucrative opportunities outside the tech industry.

For example, if you live in a rural area, many agriculture companies utilize tech and need developers. Energy companies, food, finance and insurance companies, and even call centers might need developers to support their business.

Finding large employers in all industries can help you determine which companies might have tech openings. Once you locate them, you can check their company websites or HR departments to see which positions they're hiring for.

In the next section, you'll learn some tips for contacting potential employers.

Proactively Contacting Potential Employers

It's not unusual for a company to need a new employee for some time before they get around to posting a position. This happens especially often with small companies and employers outside the tech industry. This creates an opportunity for you: If you reach out, you can raise your odds of being one of the first to apply. If you're a good fit, you might be the only candidate.

Here are the steps to take:

1. **Research your targets**: Smaller software companies or companies specializing in older technologies are great targets. They might be interested in an entry-level developer with a recent education if the opportunity comes to them.
2. **Research the company**: Look for an HR department you can reach out to, or openings listed only on their website.
3. **Find a point of contact**: For a medium-sized or large company, begin with their HR department, calling or searching online to get the name of an actual person you can email. If the company's too small for that, try to find their main telephone number or email address.
4. **Be polite and concise**: Tell them that you're a developer seeking a position, then inquire if they have any available. Don't be discouraged if they're not interested; it doesn't hurt to try, and they might even remember you when a position becomes available in the future.
5. **Follow up**: If you apply and don't get a response, follow up with a polite phone call or email to HR. Things sometimes go wrong, like an oversight in the application process or a lost resume. It's worth a call or an email to check the status of your application.
6. **Next steps**: If the company answers with a hard "no", cross them off your list. If the company sounds like they might be interested in the future, it doesn't hurt to call them again in a few weeks. Set a reminder.

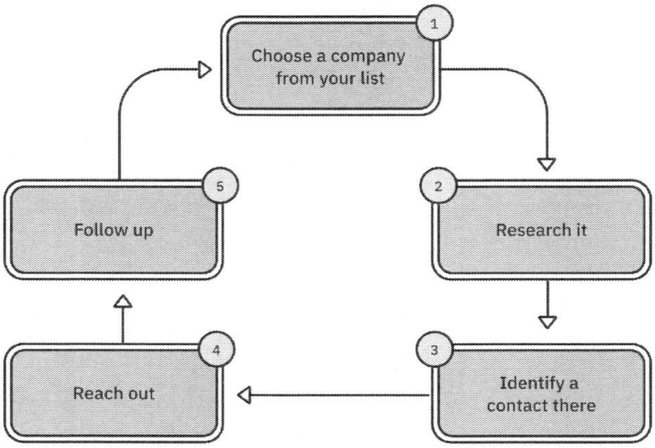

Target companies, then approach them directly.

After you've chased down all the jobs you can find to apply for, you can consider making your own opportunity.

Creating Your Own Opportunity

Aside from applying for jobs with established companies, you can consider creating your own opportunity by looking around and noticing where your skills could help. Is there a local company or organization that could greatly benefit from your skills? Could you build an app that would benefit their current system? If so, you could approach the business and ask.

To do this, research the problems that the company faces, then figure out how your skills can help them. For example, maybe you notice that a local pizza delivery company is getting complaints because customers think their pizzas take too long to arrive. Pitch them an app you could create that lets customers track their pizzas at every stage from creation through delivery, making them less anxious about the arrival time.

By showing businesses how they could profit by hiring you, you can create opportunities where none existed before.

Finally, don't forget to use one of your most valuable resources: your existing community.

Using Your Human Network

The last resource to consider is your existing human network. This can include the network you've built online, but also:

- Family members
- Mentors
- Bootcamp cohorts
- Professors
- Friends
- Local clubs
- Your faith community

Ask your network about the places they work. Do they have positions open? Do they have unmet technological needs you could help address? Do they have friends or colleagues who might be able to help? It's amazing how many people you can reach once you start asking for help.

Remember to reach out to your LinkedIn followers as well. Sometimes, simply posting that you're a recent graduate looking for a job and describing your strengths and interests is enough to open doors.

Now that you've considered a lot of your options, both traditional and nontraditional, it's important to follow up.

Following up With Leads

If you follow this advice, you could be getting leads from an overwhelming number of different places: websites, personal contacts, mailing lists and more. It's important to find a way to organize all that information.

Keeping lists is helpful. If you think a site or a contact seems promising, jot down a note or capture the link. Anytime you find a new lead, add it to this list.

Set specific times on a weekly basis to do repeating tasks like:

- Go through your list and update it. Remove leads that don't respond, turn you down or lose your interest.
- Check job sites for opportunities.
- Visit interesting company sites to check for new job postings.
- Follow up with contacts to solidify your relationships.

Note who you want to follow up with and when. These may be companies you've applied to or interesting new contacts. Following up lets employers know you were serious about your inquiry. Oftentimes, businesses are busy, which means a gentle nudge can help them prioritize your request. It's not uncommon that the proactive seeker is taken more seriously for the position.

> **Note**: Some helpful free tools for setting reminders, tracking progress and reminding yourself of when to do which tasks include Trello, Jira and Google Calendar.

Do be respectful and exercise caution when following up; you want to walk a line between showing honest interest in a position and being overzealous.

Conclusion

After finishing this chapter, you should have a good overview of how to find jobs, how to build a network of people who can help you in your career and how to follow up with the leads you discover to turn them into job prospects. Next, you'll learn how to work with recruiters to take some of the pressure of finding job opportunities off your own shoulders.

Key Takeaways

- It's important to leverage traditional resources when searching for a job.
- There are many nontraditional avenues you can try. These may give you advantages over other job seekers.
- Follow up; persistence pays.

Action Plan

- **Post your resume** on at least three job search sites.
- **Set up your LinkedIn account** and mark yourself as "open for work".
- **Research** three large companies in your area where you'd like to work. Use either the resources above or the internet.
- **Find an organization** that hires professionals with your area of expertise and reach out to them.
- **Name three tech communities** online or in your geographical area that host events that you can attend.
- **Find an event** you can attend in the next 30 days, either online or in person.
- When you attend the event, challenge yourself to **connect with at least five new people**. Exchange contact information with these individuals.
- **Identify at least one person** you know or who you can connect with online who has a career like the one you'd like to have. Reach out to them and ask them about it.
- Try out a **nontraditional job search method**.

> **Reflect on what you've learned**: Find this chapter's worksheet (PDF (https://github.com/kodecocodes/booh-materials/blob/editions/1.0/05-traditional-and-nontraditional-ways-to-find-jobs/Chapter05Worksheet.pdf)) in this book's GitHub materials repo.

Chapter 6: Working With Recruiters

By Tim Condon

Recruiters can be valuable assets to help you find your first role in tech. They've built relationships with companies and will be able to suggest roles to apply for and help you throughout the application process. However, it's important to understand their motivations and what you need to look for when meeting recruiters. A good recruiter can be a valuable contact throughout your tech career.

What You'll Learn

This chapter covers what you need to understand before reaching out to recruiters, what to look out for and how to make those connections. You'll learn:

- How recruiters work.
- How recruiters can help you.
- What to look for in recruiters.
- Where to find software developer recruiters.
- How to interact with recruiters.

You'll start by learning a bit about the tech recruiter role, so you know what their motivations to help you are.

How Tech Recruiters Work

Recruiters match up employers with employees to fill roles. They work with both sides of the job hunt and help people find work. Recruiters, or their companies, usually build relationships with companies first and are given roles by those companies to fill. They'll then reach out to their existing network or go and find people suitable to fill those roles. Some companies may even *only* fill roles through recruiters, so you won't be able to apply for those roles without them.

> **Tip**: It's worth noting that recruiters tend to focus on specific industries. So, some recruiters (or recruitment companies) will only find software engineers, while others will only find accountants, and so on. Make sure the recruiters you approach work in the tech industry!

It's important to make the distinction between **internal recruiters** and **external recruiters**. Internal recruiters work for the company that's trying to find employees; therefore, they only have jobs available within their company. External recruiters, on the other hand, work for a range of companies.

The motivations for the two types of recruiters are usually very different:

- Internal recruiters are usually full-time employees of the company and are motivated to find the best people for their open roles.
- External recruiters are usually paid a commission. This might be a percentage of the candidate's salary in the first year (once they've accepted the job) or a flat rate per role filled.

This is discussed later in this chapter, under "What to Look for in Recruiters".

This chapter primarily focuses on external recruiters, but most of the information applies to internal recruiters as well.

How Tech Recruiters Can Help You

Recruiters, especially external recruiters, provide more value than simply sending you job ads. They can give you advice, guidance and feedback to help you through every step of the job search process. After all, they want you to get the best position possible so they get paid!

The first step when you decide to work with a recruiter is to send them your resume. You'll need a resume before you go any further, so if you don't have one, read Chapter 4, "Creating a Resume & Portfolio".

Once you start working with a recruiter, ask them for feedback on your resume. They have the experience and insight into the role to know what works in a resume and what doesn't, so they'll be able to help you fine-tune it.

Once you have an established relationship and they know what kind of work you're looking for, they'll be able to offer you a range of roles to suit your skills. You can streamline the process by discussing the kind of companies you want to work for and the type of job you want. Recruiters can then flag these roles to help you find a job that's right for you.

Another common way to find roles through recruiters is to be added to their "Android developer" list or "ReactJS" list, for example. They'll send out emails with any roles that match these lists.

As you progress through the application process, your recruiter should be there to help you with each step. When you get interviews, they should be able to provide content to research and insight into the type of questions you'll be asked. They can review your resume to ensure you have enough to talk about in interviews and help you select non-tech experience to showcase your skills.

Once you've done an interview, the recruiter is usually the one to let you know the result. They'll either call you or meet with you to (hopefully!) discuss the job offer and any contract and pay negotiations. If the interview wasn't successful, they can provide feedback and areas to focus on for next time to help you improve your presentation at interviews.

Building long-term relationships with recruiters can help your career for years to come. If you find a recruiter you get on well with and trust, it's worth keeping in touch with them. As you progress in your career, if you want to change companies, then they'll be your first call.

When to Use Recruiters

Deciding when to use a recruiter doesn't have to be difficult. Remember, you can work with a recruiter while also looking for roles yourself — even if you end up finding the same role! If you want to maximize your chances of finding a great first job, then it's worth investigating both avenues.

Working with recruiters is a chance to get guidance, seek out a wide range of roles and have someone to help you as you look for your first role. When used correctly, recruiters can be a great resource.

If you're unsure, send your resume to a few recruiters and see what happens. There's no harm in seeing if they have interesting roles as you start your job search. You can also use them for advice and to check your resume. So, even if you don't plan on finding a job through a recruiter, you only need to spend a small amount of time to get some valuable benefits.

What to Look for in Recruiters

Like every field, there are good recruiters and bad recruiters. Remember, most recruiters are paid when you accept a job offer. Good recruiters will work to build established relationships with companies and find people that fit the open positions. Bad recruiters will want to fill a role as quickly as possible, no matter the suitability, so they get paid.

A good recruiter will make an effort to invest in you in the long term. They'll offer career advice, help map out goals and work with you to understand the type of role you're looking for so they can match you with a job you'll love. They won't suggest roles that aren't suitable for you.

Bad recruiters, on the other hand, might try to get you to apply for any role that's remotely relevant in an effort to secure their payday. If you feel pressured by a recruiter into applying for a role that doesn't feel right to you, then you should consider ending your involvement with them.

A bad recruiter might also try to push down salary expectations. In some cases, the recruiter is on a fixed budget and their cut is whatever you don't get paid. It's worthwhile to check the company's website or websites like Glassdoor (https://www.glassdoor.com) to see if the salaries reported by the recruiter are accurate.

Finally, a good recruiter will have a solid understanding of the tech industry. They should have insight into the basics of the different requirements and the technologies each company uses. For example, in mobile development, they should know that Flutter, React Native, Jetpack Compose and SwiftUI are all frameworks for building apps, but they're very different. You should be able to explain to your recruiter the technologies you want to work with.

How to Find Software Developer Recruiters

There are a number of different ways to find recruiters, especially in tech. LinkedIn is especially popular with recruiters, and it provides advanced search functionality to help recruiters find people. Recruiters also attend local meetups, conferences and events, so these can be great places to meet them.

Using LinkedIn

If you have a strong LinkedIn profile that's up to date and advertises that you're looking for work, recruiters will likely approach you directly. LinkedIn offers professional tools to help recruiters find people who have the skills and experience they're looking for.

To maximize your chances of being found, ensure your LinkedIn profile is up to date. The most important parts for the initial search are your **current position** and **headline**. These two pieces are the most prominent in LinkedIn's search.

Set your headline to give an overview of your desired area with **keywords** that recruiters might look for. For example, "Mobile and iOS Developer and Swift and SwiftUI enthusiast". This gives the search several keywords that help your profile get found.

Next, set your current position, closely matching your headline. For instance, "iOS and Mobile Developer specializing in Swift". You can enter your own name as the "Company Name", even if you're just building side projects. Use as many characters as you can for the best chances of being seen in a search.

In the "Skills" section, fill in all the technologies, frameworks and languages you know and use. These are usually the first keywords recruiters will search once they've narrowed down their job title.

Then, in the "About" section, write a brief description of yourself, ensuring you include keywords that recruiters might look for. For example:

> Tim is an iOS and Mobile Software Developer who has recently completed the Kodeco Developer Bootcamp. He is an experienced team player with a passion for user design and experience and has experience building iOS and web applications using Swift, SwiftUI, JavaScript and React.

This description strikes a balance between giving a brief overview of your experience and further emphasizing the keywords.

In the "Education" and "Experience" sections, add an entry for each job and educational experience you've had in as much detail as possible. Describe the projects you've worked on, the responsibilities you've had and what you've achieved. Think of it as an extended resume — everything there is searchable and might help recruiters find you.

Next, ensure you add your location so recruiters know that you're in the area they're looking to fill! Otherwise, you're severely limiting your search ranking.

Finally, make sure you add plenty of legitimate connections — this influences both recruiters and the rankings. It shows you have an established and complete profile, and you're more likely to get requests. Add everyone from your bootcamp or degree, managers and coworkers from old jobs and mentors.

Meeting Recruiters at Events

You can also be proactive in finding recruiters. You can find them by using search engines and by asking friends and colleagues for referrals.

Recruiters often attend local meetups and may even fund drinks and pizzas to encourage you to attend and build their network. Don't be afraid to approach them at these events — that's what they're there for!

Tech conferences are also a very effective way to find recruiters. Many of the companies that sponsor conferences do so to get their name out and find people to hire. The companies will send internal recruiters to meet attendees and get them interested in the companies. For more information on meetups and conferences, see Chapter 7, "Growing Your Professional Network".

How to Interact With Recruiters

Finding a recruiter to work with is the first step. The next is to interact with them professionally — which, especially for someone new to the industry, can be daunting.

In the next section, you'll learn what to expect and you'll also receive some free templates and suggestions for how to phrase your requests. Of course, use your own words and adapt them to your specific circumstances as necessary.

Reaching Out to a Recruiter

If you've found a recruiter to approach in person, go up to them and introduce yourself. Briefly describe who you are, what your background is and what you're looking for. If you're at an event where you're likely to meet recruiters, taking along copies of your resume to give to them is a good idea.

> **Tip**: See Chapter 5, "Traditional & Nontraditional Ways to Find Jobs" for tips on how to connect at events.

Don't worry about breaking the ice — they're used to talking to lots of people. It can be as simple as:

> Hi, I'm Tim. Do you have any roles to fill at the moment? I've just finished a bootcamp specializing in iOS development, and I'm looking for my first role doing that. Would you like to see my resume?

If you're introducing yourself virtually, then send them an email with a similar introduction:

> Hi,
>
> My name is Tim. I came across your profile on LinkedIn and saw you're looking to fill a number of iOS roles. I've recently completed a bootcamp specializing in iOS development, and I'm looking for my first role in that field. I've attached my resume for you to look at, and my LinkedIn profile is here.
>
> If you have any questions, then please reach out. I look forward to hearing from you.
>
> Tim

By sending your LinkedIn profile and resume, they have everything they need to add you to their lists for current and future roles.

Responding to Recruiters Who Reach Out to You

If you're in the lucky position of having recruiters approach you, then they've already done the hard part. If they're asking you for more information, or if you're interested in the role, then you can respond with the requested details:

> Hi,
>
> Thanks for reaching out to me with the role. The job description definitely looks promising, and I'd be interested in chatting with you more about it. I've attached my resume for you to take a look at. I'm free most afternoons this week if you'd like to discuss the role in more detail.

> Thanks,
>
> Tim

If you're approached with a role that you're not interested in, but the recruiter seems good, reply kindly declining the role, but mention you're interested in others. This is a good way to get added to their list:

> Hi,
>
> Thanks for reaching out to me with the mobile developer role. Currently, I'm looking for jobs that use SwiftUI and native development instead of React Native. If you have any roles that match those requirements, I'd definitely be interested in seeing those. I've attached my resume to give you some background on me, but please reach out if you have any questions.
>
> Thanks,
>
> Tim

Asking Recruiters for Help

Once you've established a relationship with recruiters, ask them for guidance on your resume and LinkedIn profile. This serves two purposes: It makes it easier for them to understand your skills and experience, and having an excellent resume also makes it easier for them to put you forward for roles.

When working with a recruiter, send them a message asking for their advice:

> Hi,
>
> I was wondering if you had any advice for tailoring my LinkedIn profile or my resume for the role that we're looking at. I want to make sure they're both as good as possible before I submit them to the company. If you could give them a look and let me know if you see anything that could be improved, that would be really appreciated.
>
> Thanks,
>
> Tim

Remember, good recruiters will help you with your resume to ensure that you're in the best possible position when they put you forward for roles. Don't worry about asking for their help!

Thanking Recruiters

Finally, if you get to the position where you've accepted a job offer — congratulations! If you want to continue working with the recruiter in the future, it's always a good idea to say thank you if they found the role for you. A thank-you email or card goes a long way toward the next time you need their help! You can write something like:

> Hi, Alice,
>
> Thank you for everything you've done to help me find my first job in tech. I really appreciate all the advice and guidance as I went through the process.
>
> I hope we'll keep in touch as I continue my career!
>
> Tim

Key Takeaways

- Recruiters can be a helpful tool when used properly, as they have a much wider network than you'll be able to build on your own. They can put you in touch with roles you might not otherwise find out about.
- Not all recruiters are good. You should be aware of their motivations and what to look out for so you can find someone you trust.
- You can find recruiters through social media, web searches, tech conferences and local events. You can also ask people in the field for referrals.
- LinkedIn is important — ensure your profile is up to date with all your experience, education and skills. Use keywords related to your field to show up in search. Also, be sure you've set your profile to "open for work" to help recruiters find you.

Resources

- Top 100 Hiring Statistics for 2022 (https://www.linkedin.com/pulse/top-100-hiring-statistics-2022-rinku-thakkar) provides some statistics on current hiring challenges.
- Recruitment Agency 101: What Does a Recruiter Do? (https://energyresourcing.com/blog/what-a-recruiter-does) explains the main roles a recruiter plays and offers another perspective on what you can expect.
- 4 Truths About Working With Recruiters (That They'll Never Tell You) (https://www.themuse.com/advice/4-truths-about-working-with-recruiters-that-theyll-never-tell-you) offers a different view of recruiters and helps explain what you should look for.
- How to Get Recruited on LinkedIn + Tips From Recruiters (https://www.jobscan.co/blog/recruiters-find-linkedin/) explains how recruiters use LinkedIn to search for candidates and what you should add to your profile to help get spotted.

Action Plan

You should now have a good understanding of what recruiters offer and how they work. Now, you can start to build those contacts to help you. Next:

- **Look for recruitment companies** in your area.
- Ensure your **LinkedIn profile is up to date**.
- **Look at local meetups or conferences** to see if they're sponsored by recruiters.
- Start **making connections**.

In the next chapter, you'll get some more insider tips on how to grow your professional network. This will help you get more job opportunities, scout companies you'd love to work for, create a network of people to ask questions when you need to and more. See you there!

> **Reflect on what you've learned**: Find this chapter's worksheet (PDF (https://github.com/kodecocodes/booh-materials/blob/editions/1.0/06-working-with-recruiters/Chapter06Worksheet.pdf)) in this book's GitHub materials repo.

Section II: Standing Out From the Crowd

The second half of this book focuses on helping you differentiate yourself from other job candidates and make a strong impression on potential employers.

"Standing Out From the Crowd" is designed to empower you to showcase your unique qualifications and demonstrate why you should be the top choice for the role among the pool of job candidates, giving you an edge in a competitive tech job market.

Chapter 7: Growing Your Professional Network

By Jennifer Bailey

You've spent the last six chapters getting tactical about your job search. Now that you know more about what you want out of a career in tech and have narrowed down the companies and roles you want, it's time to think about how to improve your chances of getting hired. A lot of people out there want to be junior devs, so how can you stand out from the crowd?

In this chapter, you'll start with a vital ingredient to success: growing your professional network.

What You'll Learn

- Why professional networking is so important.
- Who to add to your professional network.
- How to network online.
- How to network in person.
- How to maintain and grow your network over time.
- Simple soft-skills techniques for the introvert.

You'll start by learning about the value of networking and why you should put effort into it both as a junior dev and throughout your career.

Why Professional Networking is Important

You've already put a lot into your career and job search. Now, it's time to add the most important element: networking. It might surprise you to hear it, but networking is the single most effective strategy in your job search.

It's like the old saying goes: "It's not what you know, it's who you know". Success requires not only skills, but also opportunity, and networking helps you with both. The people in your network can provide valuable assistance throughout your career, but especially at the start. Some of the ways networking will help you include:

- Helping you get a better job, faster.
- Giving you a competitive edge.
- Giving you a support network that will assist you over time.

Next, you'll look more closely at each of these benefits.

Getting a Better Job Faster

Networking not only helps you get a job faster, but you'll also have a higher chance of getting a coveted position with better salary or at a more prestigious company. Meeting someone in person makes a much larger impression than simply seeing a resume. If a company gets a lot of resumes, it can help to be recognized as a face by that company, not only as words on digital paper.

Additionally, as you learned earlier, many jobs are never even listed. By getting to know insiders at a company, you're more likely to learn about new, upcoming positions that you're qualified to apply for.

Furthermore, a recommendation from a respected peer can go a long way.

Honing Your Competitive Edge

Networking improves your presentation in a job interview. It builds your confidence when talking to people within your industry, including interviewers. It helps you improve critical soft skills like communication and teamwork, which gives you an edge in an interview.

Connecting with more experienced developers can give you access to the latest industry insights, trends and best practices, which helps you stay current and relevant in the field. This gives you interesting things to talk about with your interviewers.

Unfortunately, many developers at this stage in their career don't put in the effort to build a strong network. If you do, you'll stand out clearly from other junior devs applying to the same position.

Creating a Long-Term Support Network

Networking isn't only about getting a job; it's also a way to be a good citizen in the tech arena. Just like neurons in the brain, networking in tech forms valuable connections across the entire sector. We've built a pool of collective knowledge that we all learn from and add to every day. We trade tips and techniques, we help one another solve problems and we lift each other up so we can all become better developers.

Networking helps you form valuable connections across the entire tech sector. Everyone who participates in this knowledge network is helping advance the industry.

By creating your own network, you'll have access people you can trust to ask questions and advice. You give back by helping those in your network. This makes you less isolated, gives you peers who understand your specialized field, and makes your entire career more rewarding over the long term.

Now that you understand the importance of networking, you'll learn how to get started by creating an organization plan.

Getting Organized

If you feel a bit nervous — even overwhelmed — at the thought of creating a professional network, you're not alone. But you don't need to let those feelings prevent you from using this powerful job tool.

Creating an **organization plan** helps you track your most relevant contacts and remember your next action items, without getting overloaded — or letting the pressure of socializing make you put off follow-ups. In the next section, you'll learn how to make building your network less overwhelming.

Gathering Supplies

It helps to have everything you need ready when you start networking, both in person and online.

For in-person networking this includes:

- Business cards or a printed resume (consider adding a LinkedIn QR code as described in Chapter 5, "Traditional & Nontraditional Ways to Find Jobs").
- A pen.
- A scratchpad for notes.

The pen and notepad are useful for noting down a contact's name and any interesting facts like where they work and what platforms they concentrate on. You can then transfer this information into your chosen contacts system, as described below.

Put the physical items you'll need in a designated place, so you'll always have them ready when you're out. You never know when a networking opportunity will present itself.

For online networking, you'll want:

- Handy links to your social media profiles.
- An electronic resume, or better yet, two: a formatted resume and a text version that's easy to cut and paste.
- A good headshot.

You don't have to have a professional photograph you for your headshot — though it's not a bad idea if you have the opportunity. Cell phones these days have the capability of taking such great shots that even a selfie can be professional enough.

Make sure the photo you use shows your face straight on and close enough to get a clear view. A neutral background and contrasting, solid-colored clothing is best. Use strong front lighting that shows your features well without making you squint.

Keep a good professional profile picture on hand to add to online networking sites.

> **Tip**: You can use free tools to improve your headshots. For example, Remove.bg helps you remove a distracting background, while Canva (https://www.canva.com/) gives you headshot templates that let you add frames, enhancements and even text.

Next, you'll think about how to organize your contacts once you've gathered them.

Organizing Your Contacts

Your first step is to decide the tools you'll use to organize your contacts. For example, would you prefer to use the contacts app on your phone or a physical address book? You can even use a note-taking app like Apple Notes, Google Keep, Evernote or Notion. A good note-taking tool will allow you to organize or search notes later, or to pin them if they're important.

Apps have the advantage that you're not likely to lose them easily (especially if you ensure the information in your account is backed up automatically). Some even include helpful information, like the last time you contacted a connection. A physical address book makes it easy for you to refer to your contacts, but you might not always have it when you need it.

Next, consider how you'll group your contacts. You might want to use a general group like "Job leads" or "iOS Buddies" or even "Professional Network" so you can find your professional contacts easily.

The most important data to collect is their **name**, **contact information** and a note about **where you met them** and **why** you'd like to add them to your network.

However, it's also thoughtful to keep track of the contact's **phonetic name**. Remembering how to properly pronounce someone's name demonstrates that you value them.

Finally, be sure to track **important links**. For example, associating a contact with the great talk they gave on YouTube makes it easy to remember why you wanted to connect with that person.

Whichever tool you choose to use, it's important to committing to using that tool every time. This will keep your information centralized and ensure you'll know where to find it in the future.

Now, you're ready to get down to the task of finding people to connect with and making that first contact with them.

> **Tip**: To find events and meetups both online and in person, refer to the "Networking" section of Chapter 5, "Traditional & Nontraditional Ways to Find Jobs".

Finding People to Network With

A professional network consists of the people you know in your area around you and/or on social media sites. It also includes followers you have on social media and people you know offline. Colleagues and mentors from schools or bootcamps you've attended, friends, family and community members can all be part of your network.

When building a network, quality trumps quantity. It's nice to have a large group of followers, but the most important thing is how well you interact and support one another. To that end, even a small network can be effective. It only takes one solid connection to get a lead to a great position.

> **Note**: In this section, instructions to **connect** or **add** refer to building a professional online network on LinkedIn, Twitter or any other site where developers, recruiters and companies gather. You can decide which social platforms work best for you and focus your attention there. For example, while LinkedIn is better for putting your professional self forward, many developers gather on Twitter to chat and share information, and you can definitely find job leads there.

Adding People You Know

To get started, think of the people you already know, like individuals you met in your bootcamp or education program. Add your mentors and peers straight away.

You and your peers can support one another because you have similar goals. Your mentors will support you, and they'll want to see that you succeed.

Also, add any friends or family, especially those who are in the technology field — although companies in just about every industry hire tech workers. And don't forget about people at companies where you formerly worked.

Adding Experts From Your Field

Now, add some experts from your favorite platforms and interest groups. Have you heard a talk by anyone that you liked? Follow the speaker. Are there prevalent names in your favorite platforms? Follow them. Did you read a great book or tutorial? Follow the author.

Don't worry about them being too famous or busy to be part of your network. By following experts, you'll see who else follows them. If any of those followers leave interesting comments, check them out. If they seem interesting, follow them and reach out with an interesting comment on one of their posts. This is a great way to see if there's potential to build a relationship.

Following Your Favorite Companies

Next, think of some dream employers and companies that are doing interesting things in your technology area. Follow them. If you come across recruiters or HR professionals, follow them too.

Add individuals who work for companies you may like to work for someday. Also, add folks who have a job you'd like to have someday. You can add an element of fantasy to this; ask yourself, "Whose career would I like mine to look like?".

By putting yourself around the people you admire, you can let their influence shape you. You'll learn more about how they got where they are, then use that as inspiration for your own life.

What to Avoid

There's not really a wrong way to build a network, large or small, but there are a few mistakes you can make.

For one thing, avoid spammers who waste your time and look bad if anyone checks out who you follow. Spammers are generally easy to identify as they'll approach you with unnatural-sounding messages that ask for your time to hear how their services can benefit you.

You always want to make a professional impression, so avoid negativity or controversy in the public domain. Steer clear of debates and politics whenever possible. You want your network to serve as inspiration and support, so it's also advisable to avoid negative voices, too.

Finally, remember to give as well as take. Don't place demands on new connections; instead, reach out to them with something they might find interesting or helpful. Be sure to give good advice where you can. If you can make an introduction or share interesting news that adds value for others in your connection, do so.

Start by asking for help or opportunities from your network as a whole. When you have built a true relationship is when you can reach out to individuals for specific support.

Now, you'll take a look at how to succeed with different types of networking, starting with in-person networking.

Networking in Person

In-person networking is unquestionably worth the effort. It makes more of an impact to meet people in person than to correspond online. Most importantly, just show up. You never know when your next lead is waiting for you at a meetup or event.

In-person networking events include conferences, meetups, career fairs and anywhere else you'll be surrounded by people who work in technology. Effective networking is a skill you can acquire through practice.

> **How I Started Growing My Network:** When I first started attending meetups and conferences, I was very shy. I was proud that I had convinced myself to go to events — this was a big first step for me. After attending many events in my area, I reflected that I hadn't met a lot of people.
>
> I observed my own behavior and realized that I wasn't slowing down to talk to people. I challenged myself to go a few minutes early and strategically plan where I sat. This allowed me to get a look at the crowd of folks and assess who I thought I'd have the most in common with. I then challenged myself to talk to at least three people before I left. This was tough at first, but it soon paid off. I started meeting many people, and my network started to grow.
>
> For some people, socializing comes naturally. If it doesn't come naturally to you, rest assured that many people are in the same boat — you're not the only person in the room who is outside their comfort zone.
>
> It gets easier to network over time, and by reaching out to others, you're helping them be more comfortable as well.

Succeeding at In-person Networking

When networking in person, being organized and on time with a plan can make things go smoothly, and even reduce your anxiety. As you're meeting people, remember to exchange social media handles with them.

Some of the easiest people to talk to are the ones **handing out swag** or **advertising** a business or product. These representatives expect to talk to everyone at the event.

Another potential contact is the event's **speaker**. It can be intimidating to approach the speaker after a talk, but they might well appreciate a friendly face. Give them a compliment or ask them a question on their presentation to strike up a conversation. Everyone in tech had to start somewhere, so even the experts can relate to what it felt like to learn and get their first job.

If the event has networking-specific opportunities, challenge yourself to participate. If there's a Slack or Discord channel to communicate about the event, join it and keep an eye out for new contacts there.

Don't forget to make social media posts about your experience at the event; this not only helps the event hosts get recognized for their effort, it also helps people who want to connect find you. And if potential employers check out your social media, this type of extracurricular activity looks impressive.

> **Tip**: Many events have a hashtag to use to make it easier to read posts about the event. If you don't know what it is, look around, ask the organizer or check out what other people are posting on social.

Events often have fun activities or free food, so challenge yourself to take part and get to know the other attendees there. Even if you don't find any leads that day, at least you got to learn and have fun.

As you network, let people know you're looking for work. This can be intimidating, but if people don't know what you need, they can't help. You might stumble across a company that's hiring or a recruiter this way.

> **Tip**: To find events and meetups online and in person, refer to Chapter 5, "Traditional & Nontraditional Ways to Find Jobs".

After the event ends, be sure you've added all your contacts. It's a good idea to send a friendly greeting to the new additions to your network while they still remember you. You can also post photos or links related to the event and tag those you met. This supports events and generally receives a warm reception.

Now that you know a good bit about networking in person, it's time to take a look at what you can accomplish online.

Networking Online

Networking in person isn't always easy to do, especially if you don't live in a big city or if you have personal obligations that make it hard to travel. Luckily, online conferences and communities give you opportunities to find people to connect with in your industry. In this section, you'll learn how to boost your chances of making solid connections online.

Networking Online at Events

When the COVID-19 pandemic prevented people from being able to travel or congregate safely, online events really took off. Today, they remain popular because they are less expensive to host and attend and people from around the world can do it easily.

Online events are easy to forget about, so be sure to add calendar reminders to log in on time.

Networking at an online event or conference is very much like networking at an in-person event, and you use many of the same tactics. It's easier to stay organized when attending an online event because much of the information, like the speakers' social media contacts, is posted. Be sure to add people to your network quickly, as online conferences are faster paced.

Like their in-person counterparts, online events often have networking-centric activities. The first step is to check the schedule for these sessions and attend them. Generally, this will be a breakout session in a small group. You can use chat to direct message anyone you'd like to connect with.

> **Note**: To learn more about networking during online conferences, check out "Professional Networking at Virtual Conferences: How to Connect Online (https://www.kodeco.com/30863967-professional-networking-at-virtual-conferences-how-to-connect-online)" by Kodeco Resident Author Jeff Rames.

Networking Through Websites and Communities

Websites like Reddit and various code communities let you join conversations related to job seeking. Some of these platforms have ways to contact users.

Make sure that you're not too self-serving on these communities. Along with finding job leads, you can also learn a lot about your chosen technology, get tips and advice and share your own. The more active you are, the better your chances of building a real connection.

It's important to follow the guidelines of the community, so familiarize yourself with them before you start posting.

If someone volunteers their contact information or places it in the public domain, you can add them to your network. You can also volunteer your social media handles in forums where you feel comfortable sharing.

Many platforms use AI to recommend threads and people who might interest you. Review these recommendations periodically and add the people that interest you.

Maintaining and Growing Your Network

Nurturing your network over time requires consistency. Set reminders for when to follow up with your most valuable leads if you don't hear from them; don't assume they're ignoring you. Follow up politely until you've gotten a reply. It's easy to forget to reply to messages.

Some thoughtful ideas for posts that nurture your network include:

- Congratulate your new contacts on their accomplishments.
- Publicly acknowledge your contacts if they help you.
- Talk openly about your goals, including the target companies you'd like to work for.
- Introduce your contacts to one another if the connection will help them.
- Write recommendations for people in your network.
- Clearly state the value you can bring to an organization.

If you do happen to neglect your networking for a while, you can strategically use holidays or other events to reconnect with someone you haven't talked to in a while. Be respectful of peoples' time, but reach out to them regularly. Make posts on your social media consistently and respond to your contacts' posts.

You may also decide to remove or unfollow sites or contacts that have gone stale. If you find the size of your network overwhelming, prune away some of the parts that aren't working out.

Over time, you're likely to attend events and have networking opportunities even after you have a job. Be sure to consistently grow your network even when you're not looking for a job. That way, opportunities will be there when you need them.

And if you received help from your network, pay it forward. Watch for opportunities to help someone else.

Soft Skills Tips for Networking

If networking doesn't come naturally for you, here are some simple tips to help you break the ice and communicate more effectively.

Conversation Starters

- **Think of a compliment**: Brainstorm some things that you really appreciate about someone you'd like to speak to. Did they give an awesome presentation? Do they have an admirable blog or LinkedIn profile? Sharing genuine appreciation is a great way to talk to people.
- **Ask a tactful question**: Come up with a question as an icebreaker. You could ask about their area of expertise, where they work or what their favorite thing is about the technology platform they use.
- **Learn a few work-safe jokes**: Why was the mobile phone wearing glasses? Because it lost its contacts. That may be a silly example, but a simple joke can be a great icebreaker. This can be particularly effective in a group setting or when you're striking up small talk with a new person. You could also choose a more developer-centric joke. How many types of people are there in the world? There are 10 types of people in the world: Those who understand binary and those who don't.

- **Learn some interesting facts or trivia**: Did you know that modern mobile phones carry more computing power than the Apollo 11? Or that since the year 2000 in Finland, throwing mobile phones is a sport? The distance record for men is over 110 meters and for women, over 67 meters. There's an endless array of interesting facts and trivia you can use as a conversation starter or just to brighten someone's day.

A good place to look for jokes and conversation starters is a simple Google search. You could also look at your social media channels for ideas or listen to some upbeat podcasts.

Now that you've learned some ways to start a conversation, keep the conversation going by communicating with kindness.

Communicating With Kindness

Kindness is the most important soft skill — strive to take with you in every interaction. Communicate to every individual you meet with kindness, and you'll have more meaningful interactions.

Here are some ways to convey kindness to others:

- Using appropriate eye contact. It will help the other person feel like they're being noticed and heard.
- Smile when it's appropriate — sometimes, when nervous, this is easy to forget.
- Demonstrate openness by listening to what your conversation partner has to say and keeping an open, interested demeanor.
- Be adaptable in case a change of subject or interruptions come up.
- Be thoughtful. One simple way to be thoughtful is to attribute the same importance to others' needs as you would to your own.

As Amelia Earhart said, "A single act of kindness throws out roots in all directions, and the roots spring up and make new trees." How else can you express it when you communicate with new people?

Key Takeaways

- Networking is one of the most crucial steps to getting a better job faster.
- Networking online and in person helps you quickly grow your resources.
- Think about what you can give to your network, not only what you can get from it.
- Consistency is the key to success with networking.
- Creating organization systems and using them faithfully helps you to grow your network over time.
- Growing and maintaining your network over time keeps it current and useful.
- Even if you're not an extrovert, you can utilize some simple soft skills to build a network.

Action Plan

- Start your online professional network by **adding three people you already know** to your social media contacts. Think close friends, family members or people you respect in the community.
- **Write out an organization plan**: How will you keep track of your most valuable contacts? How will you remember to follow up?
- Set a reminder to **make a new post to your social media channels** once a week. Follow up on it.
- **Attend an in-person networking event** and add three new contacts.
- **Attend an online networking event** and add three new contacts.

Reflect on what you've learned: Find this chapter's worksheet (PDF (https://github.com/kodecocodes/booh-materials/blob/editions/1.0/07-growing-your-professional-network/Chapter07Worksheet.pdf)) in this book's GitHub materials repo.

Chapter 8: Building in Public

By Jennifer Bailey

Now that you've started building a professional network, it's time to show the world what you've got! In this chapter, you'll learn about building in public: using your coding skills in ways that other people can see and use. This will give the world a sample of what you have to offer while helping you build your portfolio, your network and your confidence.

If you don't feel ready to take this step, don't worry! Showing off your skills can be intimidating, especially when you're just starting out. Skip ahead to the section on "Conquering Impostor Syndrome" for advice on getting past that feeling, then come back here and read on.

What You'll Learn

- How to find and participate in hackathons.
- How to contribute to open-source projects.
- Why to build a personal app, including some ideas to get you started.
- How to let potential employers know about your building-in-public experience.
- Tips for overcoming hesitation or imposter syndrome.

You'll start with a fun way to show off your skills and build your professional network at the same time!

Entering Hackathons and Coding Competitions

Hackathons and coding competitions offer excellent opportunities for new developers to make a name for themselves while meeting other devs in their area.

A **hackathon** is an event where developers are challenged to use technology to create a solution to a specific problem. Hackathons often involve working in a group to propose a solution to a real-world problem. They range from small and collaborative problem-solving sessions to larger competitions offering big prizes like cash, jobs and grants.

Hackathons are an awesome way to build in public and show off what you can do. They let you practice your skills, learn how to work on a team with other coders and meet people who might be a good fit for your professional network.

Plus, they're a great addition to your resume, and they give you something to discuss during an interview that can set you apart from other job seekers.

A **coding competition** is similar to a hackathon, and occasionally the two terms can overlap. However, a coding competition is generally more of a syntactical and algorithmic challenge where participants compete individually or in teams to solve difficult data structure and algorithm puzzles in a short amount of time.

Competitive coding is an art unto itself, and some programmers dedicate a lot of time and energy into climbing the leaderboards. However, you don't have to do that to benefit from competitive coding. Practice problems can help you build your resume, learn or review concepts and increase your talent for coding under pressure. This can help you in a technical interview, where you're given a code problem to work out.

Code competitions are another great way to build your professional network. You can join communities dedicated to them and also make connections among the people you meet at the competition.

Now, you'll learn some tips about how to locate and participate in hackathons successfully.

Participating in Hackathons

Many individuals are intimidated by the thought of participating in a hackathon. However, even people with no professional code experience can participate. Regardless of your background and level of expertise, you have something you can bring to a team.

Remember, hackathons aren't only about competition — they're about networking, learning new skills and bringing awareness to a solvable problem in the community.

Hackathons can take place online or in person. They usually last for a specific period of time, which might be a few hours or a couple of days. Developers join up in small groups to come up with creative solutions to problems that fit a specific theme. The solutions are judged by a panel on criteria that usually include the creativity, feasibility and impact of the proposed solution.

Some general tips for getting the most out of hackathons include:

- **Do your research**: Before the hackathon starts, make sure you're familiar with the rules, guidelines and resources you'll receive. If the theme is announced ahead of time, look into it before you start.
- **Work in a team**: Many hackathons will suggest or require working in a team. It helps to go early and mingle to select some individuals you'd like to work with. Your team is most likely to thrive if you have a diverse skill set. Look for team members who can contribute skills that differ from your own and who seem enthusiastic to participate until the end.

- **Prioritize and delegate**: Time is limited in a hackathon, so be sure to stay tightly focused on the challenge at hand. Come up with a solution together, then delegate specific tasks to each team member so that you can make as much progress as possible.
- **Pitch your idea**: In nearly every hackathon, you'll wrap up and pitch your idea. It's common that you don't fully implement your code idea, so the presentation is often the most important part. Be sure to build a wireframe of your app idea or create a thorough slide presentation to get your ideas across. Presenting gives you the opportunity to polish soft skills that you'll need in an interview. If you're uncomfortable, however, find a team member that likes to present or present together as a team, which can be less intimidating. Be prepared for the judges to ask you questions during your presentation.

Don't stop at just attending events, either. Oftentimes, event organizers need a helping hand. Reach out to the organizers prior to the event to see if you can volunteer. This will give you a front seat to the event along with the opportunity to meet more participants.

After you have experience attending and volunteering at hackathons, it's a great experience to host your own. Hosting gives you the chance to pick the themes and prizes and helps you build a community.

If you're hosting your own event, you don't need to make it too complicated. Create an event at a local coffee shop and offer small prizes — or none at all. Even a very simple hackathon will be a fun way to meet developers in your area!

Now that you know how a hackathon works, it's time to find one. You'll get some tips on that next.

Locating Hackathons

Some great websites to locate hackathons include:

- Google Developer Group (https://developers.google.com/community/gdg): Offers many chapters worldwide. You can find a number of hackathons hosted by community volunteers on a variety of topics.
- Hacktoberfest (https://hacktoberfest.com/about/): Hacktoberfest is an annual event that encourages participants to contribute to open-source projects in the month of October.

- Hackathon for Social Good (https://www.womenwhocode.com/hackathon-social-good): Women Who Code's Hackathon for Social Good gives participants the opportunity to contribute to causes that matter to them the most. You can work in a team or alone and there are many speakers and great support to engage you throughout the process.
- Major League Hacking (https://mlh.io/): Hosts lots of hackathons for students. After graduation, you can attend for 12 more months. They also have non-student hackathons.
- Devpost (https://devpost.com/): Provides a platform where hackathons host projects and create teams. Their excellent search system lets you filter by in-person or online events, topic, location, prize amount or date. This site is particularly helpful if you live outside the United States because it has a broader international community.
- Devfolio (https://devfolio.co/hackathons): Hosts some of India's largest community hackathons, as well as listing hackathons worldwide. You can search by city, time frame, application status, rating and type.
- HackerEarth (https://www.hackerearth.com/challenges/): Hosts hackathons and challenges. It's well organized, and you can filter by hackathons, competitive, university and hiring challenges. You can use this site to practice problems — and it even comes with a leaderboard so you can see how your efforts stack up.
- Eventbrite (https://www.eventbrite.com/): Eventbrite helps you find events both online and locally, which makes it a great place to find local and online hackathons. It's easy to use and you can search for events by location and keywords.
- Meetup (https://www.meetup.com/): Lists clubs and other events, including hackathons. It's a useful platform to find hackathons near you.

Next, you'll look at how to make coding competitions work for you.

Coding Competitions

Similar to hackathons, coding competitions give you the chance to build in public and make a name for yourself. A hackathon centers around proposing an idea and providing the proof of concept. A coding competition differs in that many teams are given specific code challenges that showcase logic and syntax skills.

Competing in coding competitions is an excellent way to build your interviewing skills. Oftentimes, code interviews will present algorithmic problems that the interviewee must solve in a short time frame. By practicing logic and syntax problems that center around data structures and algorithms, you'll be more prepared to tackle these challenges should they arise in the code interview.

Like any other sport, the more you practice, the more competitive you become. Coding competitions are the most fun for individuals who like algorithmic problems.

Succeeding at Coding Competitions

It takes a lot of practice to become a competitive coder. Don't be discouraged if you aren't winning right off the bat. Not only will you need a good understanding of your chosen language, but another good area of focus is **data structures and algorithms**, sometimes shortened as **DSA**. Studying DSA serves a dual purpose: This knowledge will help you ace coding interviews while also teaching you to be a fast and efficient problem solver.

> **Note**: To learn more about data structures and algorithms, check out the following books from the Kodeco library:
>
> • Data Structures and Algorithms in Dart (https://www.kodeco.com/books/data-structures-algorithms-in-dart)
>
> • Data Structures and Algorithms in Kotlin (https://www.kodeco.com/books/data-structures-algorithms-in-kotlin)
>
> • Data Structures and Algorithms in Swift (https://www.kodeco.com/books/data-structures-algorithms-in-swift)

Here are some more tips on how to boost your performance at coding competitions:

- **Lots of practice**: Start by trying many problems on your own until you know the ins and outs of a popular language used to solve them, like Java, C++ or Python.
- **Research other competitions**: Check out how people have won previous coding competitions. Work to deeply understand their code and why they made the choices they did.

- **Break down the problem**: Make sure you fully understand the challenge, then break it down into bite-sized tasks that you're comfortable tackling.
- **Optimize your code**: Efficiency counts in coding competitions, so make sure you take the time to not only come up with a solution, but also to optimize and test it.
- **Focus on learning over winning**: Especially at the beginning, it's more important to improve your skills than to win the competition. So put in a serious effort, but don't feel pressured or stressed. The more competitions you enter, the better your skills will become.

Finding Coding Competitions

So now that you know how to approach coding competitions, the next question you probably have is where to find them. Luckily, a quick Google search will show you a wealth of coding competitions. Some of my favorites come from Google itself. Here are some well-known competitions to enter:

- Google Code Competitions (https://codingcompetitions.withgoogle.com/): **Code Jam** allows you to work through rounds of puzzles — plus it offers a large cash prize. In **Hash Code**, you pick your team and solve an engineering problem together. **Kick Start** is a coding competition meant for students and those who are new to coding competitions.
- Topcoder (https://www.topcoder.com/community/arena?ref=nav): Offers weekly single-round matches, two annual tournaments and a programming and design contest.
- The ICFP Programming Contest (https://www.icfpconference.org/contest.html): Held every year, a few months before the International Conference on Functional Programming. There's no entry fee or preregistration, and you can work from anywhere and in any size team.
- Other well-known sites include: HackerRank (https://www.hackerrank.com/), CodeChef (https://www.codechef.com/), LeetCode (https://leetcode.com/), Codeforces (https://codeforces.com/) and Project Euler (https://projecteuler.net/). Another benefit of visiting these sites is that each includes practice problems.

Now that you've explored building publicly through hackathons and coding competitions, you'll learn about coding for the community.

Coding for the Community

The competitive spirit is great, but there are other ways to build your profile and code publicly. When you code for your community, you volunteer your skills to help someone you know or something you believe in — while simultaneously showcasing your work.

The best way to find opportunities is to think about where you can help out in your community. Small businesses, faith communities, local schools, sports teams and clubs of all kinds might benefit from your skills.

You can also check with online charities or causes. A variety of individuals and businesses need simple apps, basic websites or help updating existing systems. Websites such as donate:code (https://www.donatecode.com/) and Social Coder (https://socialcoder.org/) are good places to start.

Often, I come across situations where I think of easy-to-build apps that someone I know could use: a simple calculator, a flashcard game or an app with a map and company information, for example. As an aspiring dev, you could use these observations to build your portfolio.

Not sure where to start? Talking to people who own businesses or run community organizations is the best way to uncover their needs. If you're working in a job outside of tech, you might even identify a need your current employer has. I knew an individual who created a custom point-of-sale system for their company while they were in school. This led to a promotion and shifted their role from something non-technical to in-house developer and tech support.

When coding for the community, be sure to keep the time commitment and project scope realistic. Only select projects that are small and manageable. Make sure they have a finite end date, or that you can delegate them to someone else later, when you've found a tech job. You can also assess whether you can ask for payment for your contribution.

Supporting the community is a wonderful way to build in public and add to your portfolio and reputation. Plus, it always feels good to help!

Another way to contribute to the community is by working on open-source projects.

Contributing to Open-Source Projects

Open-source projects contain source code that's openly available in a **repository** — a **repo** for short — typically hosted on GitHub or sometimes GitLab. Open-source project licenses (https://opensource.org/licenses/category) let you copy and modify this code, sometimes with a requirement to credit the original project.

Contributing to open source gives you the opportunity to:

- Create code that demonstrates your ability.
- Join a community.
- Learn new skills.
- Find mentors and connections for your network.
- Improve apps or libraries you personally use.

For job seekers, it's another great way to show off your coding skills where future employers can see them.

There are many ways to contribute including, but not limited to, coding. This means that it's easy to get started at a level you feel comfortable with.

One way to start is by correcting existing documentation. Once you feel comfortable with that, you can go a step further and add new documentation.

Once you're ready to do a bit more, consider some other options:

- If you have a talent for design, create logos or improve layouts.
- Volunteer to help the community by planning events or helping with mailing lists or blogs.
- Keep an eye on the ticket queue and find duplicate issues or link to existing solutions.
- Help others by answering questions or helping them with their coding problems.
- And of course, contribute code.

A good first step when you join an open-source project is to introduce yourself. Join the discussion and chat channels, familiarize yourself with the current issues and acquaint yourself with the community leaders.

Most projects contain a license, a README that explains what the project does, a document about how to contribute, a code of conduct, and of course, the code base. Be sure to review and follow the code of conduct. Review the README and contributing guidelines thoroughly, then clone or download the project and look through it carefully. If you're having trouble building the project, review all the documentation, then ask for help.

Once you're familiar with the community, the code of conduct and the code base, look for an issue you'd like to tackle. Then, submit your contribution via a pull request according to the project's guidelines.

Now that you've learned more about contributing to open source, it's time to locate a project.

Finding Open-Source Projects

One way to find an open-source project is to think about the code libraries and products you use. Contributing to a project you value is motivating — not to mention, you'll have more insight into how to improve the project if you've used it before.

Open-source projects have a **/contribute** page that shows issues you can work with on GitHub. For example, here (https://github.com/facebook/react/contribute) is the /**contribute** page for React, which links to a detailed guide to contributing to this JavaScript UI library, originally developed by Meta.

You can also use tools like the following:

- Explore GitHub (https://github.com/explore/): Helps you find your next project, see what's trending and connect with the GitHub community.
- Open Source Friday (https://opensourcefriday.com/): Encourages users to spend a few hours on Fridays contributing to the open-source software they use. It's well organized, making it easy to find projects and issues to contribute to. It also offers communities that welcome new contributors.
- First Timers Only (https://www.firsttimersonly.com/): Links to a hands-on tutorial that walks you through contributing on GitHub for the very first time. It also has many links to help you find projects with issues that new contributors can help with.

- Up For Grabs (https://up-for-grabs.net): Lists projects actively seeking contributions.
- Good First Issues (https://goodfirstissues.com): Compiles issues labeled as a good first issue for first-time contributors.
- MediaWiki (https://www.mediawiki.org/wiki/How_to_contribute): A very cool open-source project that has help and instructions on how to participate in many capacities, including code!

Choosing an Open-Source Project

Once you've identified some projects you'd like to work on, here are some things to check:

- How recent is the project? When was the last commit?
- Are there a lot of contributors?
- How many issues are there, and when were they opened?
- Is there a discussion board, Discord or Slack channel? How active is it?
- Look over the project's pull requests. Does the community look welcoming based on the comments from maintainers?

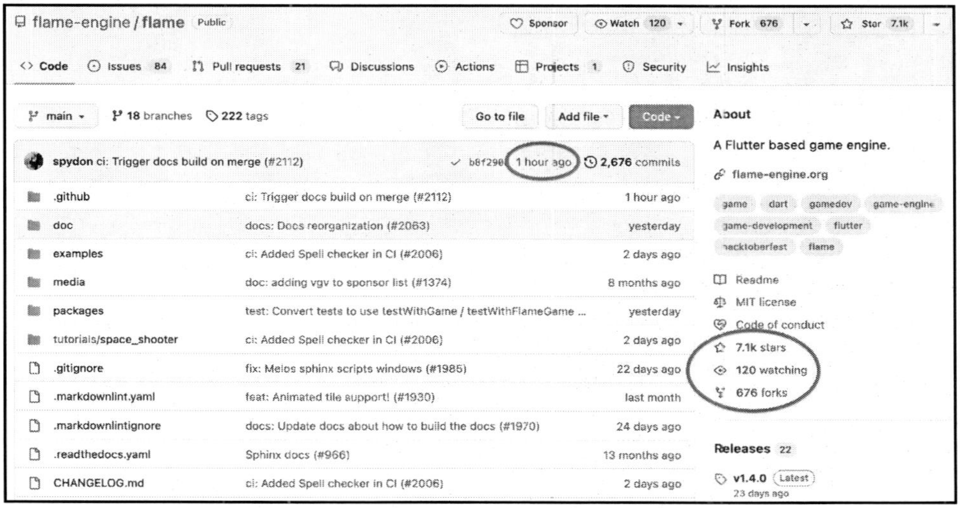

What to look for in a GitHub repo.

Using Flame (https://github.com/flame-engine/flame) as an example, here are some things to notice at the time of this writing:

- This project is active — the last commit happened just an hour ago.
- This project is popular — over 7,000 people starred it.

If you were thinking about contributing to this project, you'd also want to look at the open **Issues** (in this case, there are a lot — 84) and the **Pull Requests**. Many open pull requests may mean there aren't enough maintainers to keep up with the contributors; it's worth looking into.

You can use all of this information to decide whether a project is a good fit for your time. Open-Source Collaboration Using Git and GitHub (https://www.kodeco.com/203-open-source-collaboration-using-git-and-github) is a hands-on tutorial to help you on your way.

Contributing to open source is rewarding; you're helping the code community, building your network, showcasing your abilities and learning new skills, all at once. However, publishing your own app is another way to build in public that lets you strike out on your own.

Shipping Your Own App

A very clear way to show the world that you're an app developer is to build and publish your own app. This helps you polish your skills while giving you a concrete piece for your portfolio.

When planning your app, aim to keep your idea appropriately scoped for a team of one. Start simple with something like a to-do list, calculator or tracker, but use current techniques and tools to demonstrate that your skills are up to date. Review the big announcements from your tech stack's most recent conference, such as Apple's WWDC or Google I/O, to stay current with new frameworks.

Another way to come up with app ideas is to draw on your personal passions, like building a character guide for your favorite video game or an app to support a favorite hobby.

Keep your codebase on GitHub or somewhere else where you can share it with the world. Include a detailed README file. In the README, note all the modern features you included, and add screenshots to demonstrate what you've done at a glance.

> **Note**: An example of a beautiful README is Jeremy Freeman's Pixel-Grid app (https://github.com/freeman-lab/pixel-grid).

Since you're designing this app to act as a kind of advertisement for your skills, make sure you create a detailed GitHub profile that includes a good headshot. Include current contact information, like social media links, to make it easy for admirers to contact you.

> **Tip**: There are guidelines for how to create a good headshot in Chapter 7, "Growing Your Professional Network".

In the repo, show off your thinking by making frequent and well-labeled commits.

After you've built your app and pushed the code to GitHub, it's time to publish it! Be sure to include good screenshots that demonstrate the most technical features.

When you're done, you'll have a link to share with potential employers. Check out Publish to the Google Play Store (https://www.kodeco.com/28798254-publish-to-the-google-play-store) or Publishing to the App Store (https://www.kodeco.com/11678704-publishing-to-the-app-store) for more about bringing your app to market.

Now that you've courageously put your skills and talents out there where the world can see it, the last step is to share your accomplishments.

Sharing Your Accomplishments

Just as you'd market an app to make it sell better, you'll need to market your skills if you want people to hear about them. So remember, whenever you accomplish something, be sure to share it with the community and document it in your portfolio.

For example, when you participate in hackathons or coding competitions, share that to your social media and tell your friends. If you've earned an accolade, add it to your resume.

Create a GitHub profile README (https://betterprogramming.pub/how-to-stand-out-on-github-with-profile-readmes-dfd2102a3490) to showcase your code. See some fun examples of these profiles here (https://github.com/abhisheknaiidu/awesome-github-profile-readme).

Anything you've built for the community, added to an open-source project or published yourself can be included on your LinkedIn portfolio and your resume. When you apply for specific positions, detail your relevant accomplishments in your cover letter.

A great way to keep a log of what you've been up to is to create a blog and add a post about each of your activities. You'll be surprised how quickly they build up.

Are you ready to build in public? If you're feeling overwhelmed or nervous, the next section will help ease your mind with some tips about imposter syndrome.

Conquering Imposter Syndrome

Imposter syndrome is when a person underestimates their own skills, leaving them afraid of being exposed as a fraud. In fast-paced fields like tech, imposter syndrome is especially common, so don't worry if you feel this way. You're certainly not alone.

Feelings of inadequacy and self-doubt are often not objectively true. If you've made it this far in your career and you're representing yourself fairly to potential employers, you're not an imposter.

The bad news is that imposter syndrome happens to many, particularly when they're on the cusp of leveling up their skills and career. I personally have had many struggles with imposter syndrome and will probably have many more.

The good news is that these feelings are manageable. They might not go away entirely, but you can push back against them; you don't have to let them get in your way.

Identifying Imposter Syndrome

One of the most difficult things about imposter syndrome is that it's sneaky. It's likely to come up when learning something new, starting a new job or exposing your work to a public forum. If you're feeling hesitant or overwhelmed at the prospect, start questioning why.

Feelings of not belonging, not being quite up for the task, or that what you've achieved isn't enough are symptoms of imposter syndrome. You might be experiencing imposter syndrome if you credit your success with outside factors like luck, have difficulty accepting compliments, or have trouble enjoying what you've achieved. Really question those thoughts and feelings, because they're very likely not true.

Managing Imposter Syndrome

If you are having these feelings, here are some tips to help you:

1. Realize What You're Feeling Is Common

A lot of developers struggle to feel *smart* or *qualified* enough because tech is a high-pressure, ever-changing environment. The job descriptions and demands of each new project are often unpredictable. The pressure of always needing to learn the latest changes in your platform can make you feel like you're always behind the curve.

Remember, however, that all developers face these challenges. Embrace the learning process, remember you have your own strengths and focus on progress, not perfection.

2. Look for Support

Many people experience imposter syndrome, but they don't always talk about it. Find individuals you trust in your network and ask for support. With a solid professional network, you're sure to find people who can help you overcome your challenges and empathize because they've been there themselves.

3. Inventory Your Accomplishments

It's good to acknowledge shortcomings and to keep an objective view, but be sure to acknowledge accomplishments too. Recall times you've been consistent, dependable, trustworthy and helpful. Make a list of your strongest attributes.

The idea isn't to inflate your ego! Rather, listing your accomplishments helps to combat the negative filter that so commonly accompanies imposter syndrome. It's easy to focus on one mistake, even when you've had a dozen successes. Celebrate your accomplishments and look back at them often.

4. Ask for Feedback

Many times, we write stories in our heads about our skills or perceived failures. Don't assume these stories are true; instead, ask mentors, managers or peers for objective feedback. You might be surprised that they have a more positive view of your aptitude and performance. I'm often surprised that feedback from others is more positive than I anticipated.

5. Let Go of Expectations

Unrealistic expectations feed imposter syndrome. Sometimes these come from outside, but often they're from inside. Know you're exactly where you need to be. Remind yourself that outcomes are often unpredictable, so don't get too attached to the end result you visualized. One of my favorite sayings in college was "Hope for the best, prepare for the worst and take what comes".

6. Let Go of Perfectionism

Learning often happens through mistakes, and code projects are rarely straightforward from beginning to end. Unforeseen difficulties arise, and you must adapt. Focus on moving forward. Remember that it's easy to get caught up in feeling like you need to be an expert in everything. Instead, focus on making progress and building new skills.

7. Cultivate a Spirit of Play

Placing high stakes on tasks makes them scarier to accomplish. Instead, take some of the pressure off by finding ways to make your work more fun. For example, you could think of learning as a quest or use your sense of humor to put your goals into perspective.

8. Do It Anyway

Fear is just an emotion. Think of a picture of a tiger — imposter syndrome can't tear off the page and attack you, although your body might feel like it's under that kind of threat. Take a few deep breaths, do what you fear, then walk away and find a distraction.

You might be surprised to find that your work is better received than you think! If not, you'll collect valuable feedback for next time.

When dealing with imposter syndrome, the best thing you can do is educate yourself. Be prepared for when it's likely to happen. You don't have to stop the emotions, just recognize them and proceed — the feelings will pass.

> **Note**: For some good imposter syndrome resources, check out the websites of the International Society for Imposter Syndrome Studies (https://impostorsyndrome.com/) or the American Psychological Association (APA) (https://www.apadivisions.org/division-28/publications/newsletters/psychopharmacology/2017/11/imposter-syndrome).

Key Takeaways

- Building in public is a great way to learn while expanding your portfolio and network.
- Showcasing your skills is key to getting great opportunities.
- You can demonstrate your skills by participating in hackathons, working on open-source projects, building your own apps and more.
- If you're nervous about showing off your skills, don't let imposter syndrome stop you from reaching for your aspirations.

Resources

- Take up Coding Challenges to build your skills (https://consultadd.com/technology/take-up-coding-challenges-to-build-your-skills-in-2022/) rounds up major international coding competitions. HackerEarth (https://www.hackerearth.com/challenges/), mentioned earlier in "Locating Hackathons", also lists upcoming coding competitions for a wide variety of languages and tech stacks.
- What it means to contribute (https://opensource.guide/how-to-contribute/#what-it-means-to-contribute) from the Open Source Guides (https://opensource.guide) curated by GitHub. This guide, which itself is open source, provides detailed guidelines on all aspects of creating, maintaining and contributing to open-source projects.
- Art of README (https://github.com/hackergrrl/art-of-readme). This guide to writing a great README links to examples and references. It also includes a checklist to help you cover all the bases when creating your own repository or improving the README in an existing project, which can be a great way to make an initial contribution!

Action Plan

- Find and **participate in a hackathon**.
- **Try out three code problems** from one of the code competition sites.
- **Brainstorm a simple app** that you could write for an individual, club, small business or organization in your community. Draw a rough mock-up.
- **Find an open-source project** you'd like to contribute to and join the community.
- Look for one **open-source issue you can resolve**.
- Brainstorm a simple app that you can **build and publish yourself**.
- Add a project you've done in school or as a hobby to **GitHub and include a great README**.
- Write down at least **three accomplishments in the tech field** that you're proud of.

> **Reflect on what you've learned**: Find this chapter's worksheet (PDF (https://github.com/kodecocodes/booh-materials/blob/editions/1.0/08-building-in-public/Chapter08Worksheet.pdf)) in this book's GitHub materials repo.

Chapter 9: Learn & Share

By Jennifer Bailey

In the last chapter, you explored ways to share your hard-earned coding skills. Now, you'll continue to use your skills to make an impact on your community while simultaneously building your resume and network.

You'll learn how to learn and share by keeping your skills sharp, then sharing what you learned with your community. If you think that no one can learn from a developer at your experience level, remember that no matter where you are, others are striving to get as far as you've already come. You can give them a helping hand.

Now, it's time to lift while you climb.

What You'll Learn

- Why learning and sharing is a powerful strategy to boost your skills and network.
- How to determine the next valuable skill to learn to add to your resume.
- Simple tips to share knowledge with your community.
- How to share your knowledge through technical articles, tutorials and videos.
- Tips for giving presentations at conferences and other events.
- How to find or create mentoring opportunities.

First, you'll look at why sharing what you learn through mentoring is so important.

How Learn-and-Share Helps Software Developers

Think back on your learning experiences in tech. Can you remember a time you struggled to learn a fundamental coding concept? Did someone help you out by walking you through the concepts you needed to understand? If not, do you wish someone had? Well, now you get to be that person.

Because of the ever-evolving nature of tech, one constant in your career is that you'll always be learning. By being strategic about what you learn and how you share it, you can stand out from the crowd, regardless of your experience level.

Learning and sharing can boost your career in three important ways:

- It helps you internalize what you learn.
- You boost your resume and position yourself as a knowledgeable person in your field.
- Supporting other developers helps advance your industry as a whole.

You'll take a quick look at each of these benefits next.

We Learn Better When We Teach Others

As the saying goes, to learn something, do it. To master something, teach it.

We often think that teachers have to be experts in their field. However, studies show that when students teach other students, they learn the subject better. Psychology Today calls this phenomenon the protege effect (https://www.psychologytoday.com/intl/blog/how-be-brilliant/201206/the-prot-g-effect). This is true even in cases of grade-school students tutoring their classmates or older Montessori students teaching younger ones.

When people know they'll be teaching a subject, they pay more attention, remember it better and apply it more effectively.

You can take advantage of the protege effect by sharing what you learn with other developers. Even if it's not an advanced topic, there are other devs out there who can benefit. While helping those around you to achieve their goals, you'll be learning skills and advancing your own career.

Building Your Resume by Teaching

As you learned in Chapter 1, "Evaluating Your Options", eagerness to learn is an important hiring criterion, especially for junior devs. Demonstrating that you consistently learn new things and share your knowledge will impress potential employers. It's a great way to flesh out your resume and gain exposure for your hard-earned skills.

Additionally, teaching demonstrates other highly valued skills, like a true mastery of a subject and the willingness to lead and assist a team.

Plus, you'll have the opportunity to add a community of supportive learners to your network. It also feels good to pay forward the mentoring you've received, and you'll set an excellent example for those who follow in your tracks.

Advancing Your Industry

As developers, it's important to support one another in our communities so our platforms can keep moving forward. Mentorship is the opposite of gatekeeping knowledge, which is harmful to tech communities as a whole. By helping others learn, you promote diversity and inclusion, which can lead to a more robust platform.

Additionally, teaching at any level improves the overall level of technical proficiency within the community. This can lead to the creation of better-quality software, which attracts more users and developers to the platform.

Ready to get started? First, you'll explore what topics you'd like to learn and share.

Selecting a Programming Topic to Learn and Share

So, what should you learn next? Start with the skills and platforms you already know. Have they had a recent update or feature? What's up-and-coming in beta that the community is buzzing about? Have there been any announcements from the vendor? If so, these can be excellent topics to dive into.

What about the apps that are already in your portfolio? Can you augment them with a new trend in the platform? This will keep your portfolio evolving. In the case of iOS apps, including a new framework might even get your app featured in Apple's App Store!

Consider the following as you brainstorm:

- Check **job postings** for required and recommended skills both at your level and the level above you. Popular skills like unit testing or debugging can be good topics to learn and share.
- Review **recaps** of the most recent vendor conferences for your tech stack, whether that's WWDC, Google I/O or something else. You can find these on Kodeco and other trusted tech sites. See this chapter's "Resources" section for links.
- Consider **frameworks** or other questions that come up frequently on developer Discords, Slacks or Meetup discussions.
- Think about **what you learned** from your most recent project or pull request, especially if you struggled a bit.
- Which **features** show promise of being popular in the future? Look around Reddit and platform communities to see what's exciting developers right now.
- Dive into **topics that interest you**. Learning is easier when you're excited about your topic.

Where to Research Tech Topics

When selecting a topic, check if it has good documentation. If not, that could be an opportunity for you. Look for tech blogs on Medium, code labs from Google and educational materials from Apple. A topic is more difficult to learn if it doesn't have good documentation or code examples — but you're also likely to get more attention.

Here are some other places to research:

- The canonical source for understanding a coding framework or concept is the implementation itself, so look at the code for the framework you're learning.
- Going up one level of abstraction, read the developer documentation straight from Apple, Google or whoever created the framework.
- Look for tutorials and articles on respected tech learning sites like Kodeco.
- Search YouTube and Vimeo for conference talks and other videos on your topic.

Once you've selected a topic and started your research, it's time to share with the world as you learn.

So, now that you know how to find the topic you want to learn, the next question is how to put yourself in a position to teach it. Even as a beginner, you have many options to share as you're learning. In this chapter, you'll cover:

- Sharing through the community.
- Teaching through online publications.
- In-person mentorship.

You'll start with sharing what you know within your tech community.

Learning and Sharing With Your Community

Sharing what you've learned with your community doesn't have to take a lot of time or effort. In fact, you might come across ways to do so as you research questions or study interesting topics.

Here are a few easy places to start:

- **Answering questions on Stack Overflow**: New features often have many questions about them that haven't been answered yet. This gives you an opportunity to share what you've learned.
- **Providing feedback about the platform**: You can provide direct feedback about the feature to the company that maintains the platform. You can also post in forums if the vendor provides them, like Apple does at https://developer.apple.com/forums/.
- **Conversing with the community**: You can discuss the feature in platform-specific communities on Slack, Discord, Reddit, Mastodon, Twitter and LinkedIn. You can ask questions, provide support and find camaraderie among your peers.

Another powerful way to share what you're learning and help others along the way is by publishing your takeaways. In the next section, you'll learn some ways to do this.

Publishing What You're Learning

Publishing what you've learned gets your name out there, attracts people to join your network and makes you more attractive for employers. Here are some ways that you can do this.

Creating a Tech Blog

One way to share is to create a blog, which is also a great place to house your portfolio. You can register a domain and purchase hosting with a company like Bluehost (https://www.bluehost.com/), then use a tool like WordPress (https://www.wordpress.org) to publish your blog.

There are also several free or affordable platforms you can use, like:

- Kodeco (https://www.kodeco.com/11455688-write-for-us): If you have strong technical and writing chops, you can apply to be a writer at a tutorial site like Kodeco. You don't have to build your own audience, and you get paid for sharing what you learn.
- Medium (https://medium.com): Medium is free for writers, although you can choose whether to put articles behind a paywall for readers. It's prominent in tech and comes with a built-in audience.

- LinkedIn (https://www.linkedin.com/): It's not as obvious, but LinkedIn posts can be very much like a blog, and easy to attract an audience. To use LinkedIn as a blog, just create a post. This is a powerful place to write articles about what you're learning.
- Wix (https://www.wix.com/): Wix is a wonderful way to create a free blog and website. It doesn't come with an audience, but it requires no previous experience with building a blog. The free plan allows a significant amount of mileage.
- Publish (https://github.com/JohnSundell/Publish): This static site generator lets Swift developers write websites in their favorite language. Learn more about how to use this for your blog in this chapter's "Resources" section.

Be sure to post a professional profile on your blog along with technical articles about what you're learning. This comes in handy if recruiters or anyone seeking tech talent stops by.

> **Note**: Creating a blog can be the beginning of something great. Here's the inspiring story (https://www.kodeco.com/36804029-kodeco-podcast-ray-and-matt-explain-it-all-podcast-vol2-s1-e1) of Ray Wenderlich, the Kodeco site founder who started by learning and sharing his mobile app knowledge on a blog!

Writing Influential Tech Articles

Once you've set up a blog, you can fill it with excellent tech articles. The beauty of having a blog is that you can use it however you like. You can create articles about what you're learning currently, the problems you've encountered and how you solved them or an overview of a technology topic.

When writing a tech article, here are a few things to keep in mind:

- **Consider the audience**: Imagine your ideal audience and write for them. This can be other developers in your sphere, juniors on your dev team and/or potential employers. Write the article specifically for them and keep in mind which topics they'd like to read about.
- **Keep the language simple**: Shorter sentences and simpler words help readers understand your writing. This will also help your article achieve higher SEO readability scores.

- **Use screenshots, code snippets and illustrations**: An article with examples, graphs and illustrations pops. It helps readers understand the concepts you're demonstrating.
- **Create an outline**: Organize your thoughts by creating a simple outline. Write transitions between each section as you fill in the outline with paragraphs.
- **Design for readability**: Make sure the blog is accessible (https://mediablog.prnewswire.com/2022/10/05/blog-accessibility-tips/) by filling in content tags on the images and ensuring it's easy to navigate.
- **Keep points concise**: Each paragraph should contain one main point. The article doesn't have to be wordy to impress. Avoid your writing being deemed Too Long; Didn't Read (TL;DR).

You can go beyond articles by creating step-by-step tutorials by incorporating screenshots and using code formatting tags or gists from GitHub. Most blog tools include plugins for code formatting, like this one for WordPress (https://wordpress.org/plugins/syntaxhighlighter/). There's also this interesting tool (https://github.com/googlecodelabs/tools) that can help you create a tutorial that looks like a Google Code Lab. You can also use a tool as simple as Keynote, Google Docs or PowerPoint.

The tool isn't as important as the content, so don't get too hung up on the formatting. The overall goals are to be able to distribute and share your tutorial and make it easy to read and navigate.

Some ways to make your step-by-step tutorials even more helpful include:

- Add images and highlighted code snippets.
- When possible, present the code snippets as text that can be cut and pasted.
- Attach a sample project or post a link to a sample project in GitHub so your readers can review the code.

Another way you can present a code tutorial is by recording videos.

Recording Tech Tutorial Videos

Few things capture the attention of a crowd more than a live coding demonstration. Today, it's extremely easy to create interesting videos without a lot of extra investment in tools.

Here are some popular tools for recording video tutorials:

- YouTube: This is probably the simplest platform for publishing video tutorials.
- Screencast-O-Matic (https://screencast-o-matic.com/): A reasonably priced cross-platform tool for screen capture and hosting videos.
- QuickTime or iMovie: These let you do simple screen captures on a Mac.
- ScreenFlow (http://www.telestream.net/screenflow/overview.htm): A more professional Mac video creation tool.
- OBS Studio (https://obsproject.com/): A free, cross-platform screen capture tool.

You don't even need to appear onscreen to create good video tutorials. Any tool that allows you to record your voice while capturing the screen will do. If the tool allows simple editing like cropping segments, even better. Fancy features are nice, but a good video tutorial is more about the content, so a simple tool that's easy to use will suffice.

Once you've decided on a tool, it's a good idea to create an outline and a script. Create an outline first to decide how you'll break down the tutorial into steps. If you have theory sections to explain concepts, creating some Google Slides or a Keynote presentation can be handy for illustrations.

> **Tip:** You can use an AI like ChatGPT (https://chat.openai.com/) to help you create video scripts from a prompt quickly.

To make your video tutorial more professional, add free background music from the audio library within YouTube Studio or from a site like Free Music Archive (https://freemusicarchive.org/).

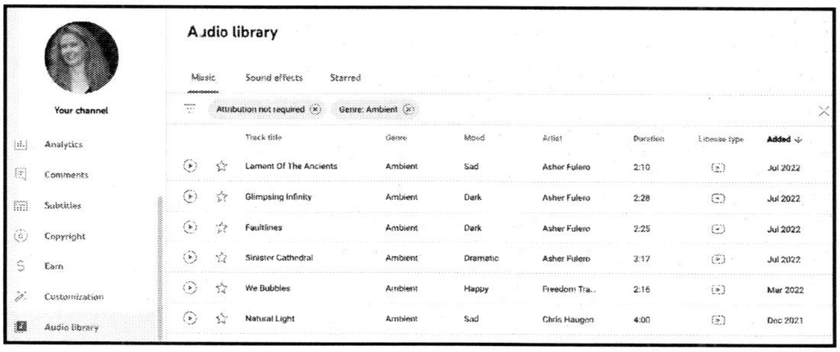

Find background music for your coding tutorial right within YouTube Studio.

Now that you've gathered the tools, you're ready to record. A simple way to create a tutorial is to start building a project, pausing between steps. You can do this in a live code fashion if you can talk and code at the same time, or record the steps and add the audio separately from a script. You can make your tutorial as formal or informal as you like.

Instructional Video Tips

Some tips for creating a great video tutorial are:

- Follow an outline or script and build a project one step at a time, explaining each step after you've added the code.
- Clearly indicate where you're adding or deleting code.
- Speed up the segments when you're typing, but have a long pause when the code segment is complete so the viewer can easily pause the video.
- Rehearse building the project first.
- For easy navigation, clearly mark each step of the tutorial with a text slide. You can add chapters later in YouTube Studio.
- Be sure to show all the relevant code on the screen slowly enough that the viewer can pause the video to find the snippet they're looking for.
- Avoid horizontal scrolling.
- Transcribe your videos.
- Build and run the tutorial after every milestone in the project.
- Use illustrations for theory sections. When explaining the theory, you can appear on camera.

Coding tutorials are helpful and engaging for the community. They're a great way to illustrate your thought process, show your personality and help learners while building your portfolio.

Whether you choose to write or record, the number one ingredient to creating great tutorials is practice. Focus on the content and avoid perfectionism. The more you practice, the better your content will become over time!

Now that you've learned about sharing your content online, you'll learn about presenting your learning in person.

Giving a Technical Presentation

Preparing a **technical presentation** is a great way to gain exposure while learning a new skill. It requires a degree of courage, but don't worry, it gets easier over time — and there's hardly a better motivator to learn a topic.

You don't need to have prior experience to present a topic. The beauty of being a presenter is that it helps you look like an expert, even when you're just learning, like everybody else.

The first step to becoming a great speaker is creating a presentation.

Creating a Useful Presentation

You'll usually need to make a slide deck for your technical presentation. You can use tools like Keynote, PowerPoint or Google Slides to create your deck.

As a bonus, you can have a sample project ready and demonstrate some live code. Be sure to thoroughly test and rehearse any live demos so you are prepared to handle anything that goes wrong. It's common to make an error while presenting or have your demo fail unexpectedly. If this does happen, just take it in stride and move on to your next slide or begin taking questions from the audience.

Building a Great Tech Talk Slide Deck

Consider the following when you're preparing your slides:

- Keep your presentations to around 20 to 30 minutes, which works out to 10 to 15 slides.
- Clearly communicate the value of your topic and how it benefits the audience.
- Grab your audience's attention with a question, an analogy or a joke.
- Cater to the least knowledgeable in your target audience.
- Use a large font and plenty of contrast on your slides.
- Provide your social media handles. Consider using QR codes so your audience can easily follow you.
- Have proof of concept in an app you can demo live. Provide a link to your GitHub project for those who'd like to experiment or learn more.

Delivering a Great Tech Talk

Some tips for creating and delivering a great presentation are:

- Elaborate on each point rather than just reading the slides.
- Use note cards or speaker notes to help you stay on track and hit all your main points.
- Make eye contact with the audience.
- Be prepared to answer questions. If you don't know, refer audience members to where they can find more information.
- Speak authoritatively. Even if you don't feel confident, act as though you are!
- Record your presentation to post on YouTube. Watch it later to learn what you did right and what you can improve.

Once you're ready to deliver your presentation, practice makes perfect. A great place to start is delivering your presentation to a small audience.

Finding an Audience

To rehearse your presentation, reach out to local meetup groups and clubs. See Chapter 7, "Growing Your Professional Network", for tips on finding these. You could also deliver your presentation to a local university, community college, code camp or even a high school. These venues often need speakers, and they provide a smaller audience to practice on.

Each time you deliver your presentation, incorporate feedback and make improvements. Your delivery will get smoother and easier every time.

Once you've mastered your topic and polished your presentation, it's time to deliver it at a larger venue like a tech conference.

Writing a Conference Talk Proposal

To present at a tech conference, you'll need to research the conference and watch for its call for papers, also known as a **CFP**. Refer to Chapter 7, "Growing Your Professional Network", for more about conferences.

Once you know which conference you want to present at, research its audience and consider whether your topic is a good fit. Think of ways to tailor your presentation for that specific conference. Brainstorm how to engage the audience in a unique way.

> **Tip**: For inspiration, watch technical presentations on YouTube and take note of what you liked best about each talk. Think about how to incorporate a similar style in your presentation.

When writing your proposal, look over the conference's call for papers carefully. They'll often provide the selection criteria along with the format and deadline to submit your proposal. Read these rules thoroughly and tailor your proposal accordingly.

The headline is the most important part of the proposal — it's what will draw an audience to your talk, so be sure yours catches attention.

Provide your bio and background on the topic. Provide a link to your presentation, any associated code projects and a video of your talk from an earlier presentation or rehearsal. Because you've done your research, include how you plan to engage their specific audience.

Be sure to submit the proposal on time, then be prepared to wait. It takes some time for the selection process to play out.

Once you've written one proposal, you can modify it and submit it to multiple conferences. Don't give up if you're not selected — this process can take some practice and time.

By this point, you've learned a lot about how to share as you study. The last way you'll explore to learn and share is through mentoring.

Teaching and Mentoring Junior Devs

Being a mentor is one of the most rewarding ways to learn and share. You can have a huge impact on someone's life and career — and it feels terrific seeing someone you've mentored succeed. In the process, you'll gain valuable skills and exposure for your own career.

There are endless ways to mentor and teach. If you've recently graduated from a bootcamp or educational program, you can start by seeking to be a mentor at your alma mater.

Assisting or Running a Coding Bootcamp

If you've graduated from a bootcamp, you've made it through the experience and curriculum. You're in a great position to help the next generation of students.

Here are some ways you can use bootcamps as a way to learn and share:

- Volunteer to work as a **bootcamp mentor**.
- Create your own mini-bootcamp by teaching Android Code Labs (https://developer.android.com/courses) or Apple's app development curriculum (https://www.apple.com/education/k12/learn-to-code/).
- You can lead a book study for a beginner text like Android Apprentice (https://www.kodeco.com/books/android-apprentice) or SwiftUI Apprentice (https://www.kodeco.com/books/swiftui-apprentice).
- Set up a bootcamp for younger developers through Code.org.
- Ask community clubs, high schools, universities and community colleges if they'd be interested in a code camp or if they have activities where they need an instructor to lead one.

If you don't have time to run an entire course or bootcamp, consider volunteering for a shorter event like a hackathon.

Judging or Volunteering at a Hackathon

In Chapter 7, "Growing Your Professional Network", you learned how to find hackathons, which are usually run by volunteers. You can reach out to local hackathons to see if they need volunteers to mentor participants, run the event or be a judge.

Hackathons often also need panelists to help determine the winner. This is a great learning experience, as you'll have to review ideas and projects as well as provide feedback to the participants.

Offering Online Office Hours

If you like to mentor from the comfort of your own home, try setting up a schedule on Calendly (https://calendly.com/) for online office hours. You can then share your calendar in your online communities and on LinkedIn. Tell learners in the community that you're willing to answer their questions on certain topics or platforms or at a certain level, and allow them to come to you for help.

By doing this, you're showing a willingness to lead and help your community. You're also advertising the skills you have to offer.

You'll be able to practice your skills by helping others and learning from them as well. You're also making yourself available for individuals, including potential employers, to talk to you directly about your skills.

Teaching or Tutoring Coding at Schools

Depending on your education, you may be able to teach a course at a community college or high school. Generally, the Higher Learning Commission or similar authority for a state or region will dictate what qualifications teachers must have. However, for a part-time instructor or a programming teacher, the school might be able to obtain a credential, as coding teachers are in short supply.

Another option is to tutor students in programming skills. Reach out to local schools and ask if they have any part-time tutoring opportunities.

Congratulations on making it through this chapter on learning and sharing. At this point, you have a solid idea of how you can use your enthusiasm for learning new things about your chosen technology to give back to the community while making a name for yourself.

Key Takeaways

- Sharing while you learn helps build your skills while enhancing your portfolio.
- Mentoring strengthens your network.
- Presenting what you learn motivates you to learn new things.
- Teaching what you've learned solidifies your own understanding.
- You can build your portfolio while creating helpful resources for others in tech.

Resources

- Learn more about writing in 7 powerful tips to write tech articles (https://www.awkbit.com/en/blog/7-powerful-tips-write-tech-articles).
- Check out Kodeco's summaries of Google I/O (https://www.kodeco.com/34078194-google-i-o-2022-recap-top-5-takeaways-for-android-devs) and WWDC (https://www.kodeco.com/34525075-wwdc-2022) for tech topic ideas.
- Want to use Swift for your personal blog? Learn how in Danijela Vrzan's How to Create a Personal Website in Swift using Publish (https://www.danijelavrzan.com/posts/2022/06/create-portfolio-website-using-publish/).

Action Plan

- **Start a developer blog** and add a two- or three-paragraph career profile in a post or in an "about" section.
- Come up with a **topic for a tech talk or workshop** that you could create.
- Reach out to three clubs, communities or educational institutions to ask if they would allow you to **present your talk or workshop**.
- Find one question on the internet related to development and **post an answer** to it.
- **Brainstorm three ways you could be a mentor** in your community — either locally or online.

Reflect on what you've learned: Find this chapter's worksheet (PDF (https://github.com/kodecocodes/booh-materials/blob/editions/1.0/09-learn-and-share/Chapter09Worksheet.pdf)) in this book's GitHub materials repo.

Chapter 10: What to Do if You're Still Not Landing Interviews

By Jennifer Bailey

After you've invested the time and energy to go through all of the steps in this book, it's natural to hope that you'll land an interview for your dream job right away. Unfortunately, the road to success isn't always a straight line. Creating a career, like creating an app, is an iterative process.

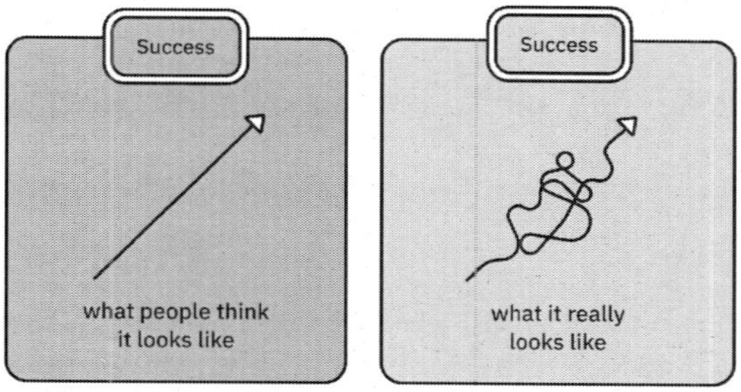

Success is rarely a straight line. There are often many twists and turns along the way.

It's totally OK if you aren't getting the interviews you hope for. It's possible that you're just facing a crowded job market and you need to stay the course, or it could be that your presentation is missing the mark and you need to make some changes. How do you know the difference? This chapter will help.

In this chapter, you'll learn how to take a closer look at your process, improving your chances of getting chosen for an interview. You'll take another look at your resume and portfolio, learn about some common mistakes that applicants make and get tips for stepping up your game. You'll also learn how to manage your emotions and make a longer-than-expected job hunt sustainable.

What You'll Learn

- To identify common mistakes that job applicants make and learn strategies to avoid them.
- How to request feedback and implement it in your application process.
- Tips to make yourself a stronger applicant.
- The importance of managing your emotions during a long job hunt and learn strategies for making it sustainable.
- How to implement a continuous improvement process for your job search.

You'll start by learning about common job application mistakes to ensure you're not making any of them.

How to Recognize and Avoid Common Job Application Mistakes

Many times, there's only a razor-thin difference between getting a call for an interview and being passed over. That difference may come from a common mistake you don't realize you're making. In this section, you'll learn many of these easy-to-make errors and how to troubleshoot your approach to make sure you're not doing them.

1. Not Tailoring Your Resume for the Position

Some people send the same resume every time they apply for a role. There are even services that will send a generic resume to open roles automatically. This is, however, a terrible tactic.

Hiring managers review dozens, or hundreds, of candidates. If they can't see at a glance why you could be perfect for the job, they'll pass you over.

Make sure that you word your resume to exactly match the qualifications your potential employer has listed. As a developer, you know the tech lingo and can easily recognize different wording for the same thing. However, an HR person scanning a resume or an automatic system that's looking for specific keywords won't know any variations and will pass you over, even when you're qualified, if you aren't using the terms they're looking for.

Check the job postings to find out what keywords they're looking for and use that wording whenever possible.

2. Not Sending a Customized Cover Letter

A cover letter is your chance to pique your potential employer's interest, so it's important to get it right. Keep them focused and to the point, and don't be shy — you want them to have an impact. Talk yourself up and show a bit of personality.

The nature of the cover letter is to catch the employer's attention. It's your chance to highlight qualities that aren't expressed as clearly in a resume, particularly if you don't yet have developer experience. Tell them who you are, what you've done, what benefit you can bring to their team and how passionate you are.

Sometimes, there's a tendency to downplay the cover letter to avoid bragging or sounding too eager. Be honest but not humble. Create a well-crafted sales pitch. The product you're selling is yourself — a dedicated and capable junior developer. End the letter with a positive call to action to get in touch with you.

Your cover letter should fit on one page. You can use a similar formula with each application, but be sure to tailor them to each company and to write them as if you were talking directly to the employer.

Include the following sections:

- What you're applying for and how you heard about it.
- Why you're so enthusiastic about the position and why your talent is a perfect fit. This takes some research. Do the research.
- What your qualifications are and how you got them.
- Experience you have that's relevant to their team.
- Personal attributes you have that will make you a great team member.
- How they can contact you and that you'd cordially invite them to do so right away.

Written correctly, your cover letter will ignite employers to action. They may see the confidence and enthusiasm reflecting through and want to give you a chance. This can set your resume apart.

3. Your Resume Isn't Easy to Scan

As mentioned above, the person who decides whether to advance you to the next step or not is very busy. You need to ensure that they can scan your resume so they can see the information they need at a glance.

Take out your resume and revisit Chapter 4, "Creating a Resume & Portfolio". Make sure that you've followed the suggested structure.

Also, to double-check your resume:

- Ensure your most relevant experience and knowledge appears at the top.
- Add any new skills you've gained, new projects you've worked on, etc.
- Give it a critical look. Is it clear but succinct? Is the font easily readable? Did any typos slip in? Can you see the most important information at a glance?

4. Not Optimizing Your LinkedIn Account

Today, many companies and recruiters find their candidates through LinkedIn. If your LinkedIn account isn't optimized — or if you don't have one at all — now's the time to get it in shape.

First, review Chapter 6, "Working With Recruiters", for tips on how to create an effective LinkedIn profile. You'll also find tips for choosing a great profile picture in Chapter 7, "Growing Your Professional Network".

Once you've set up a professional profile, make sure that it reflects good keywords for your desired role.

Recruiters and employers search LinkedIn using keywords. When you include these keywords in your LinkedIn profile, you'll show up more often in those searches.

The best place to find keywords is on job postings themselves. However, you can also mine the profiles of folks who already have jobs like the one you're trying to land. Look at the keywords in their profiles and see which ones you might legitimately include in your own.

The first place to put keywords is in the **headline**: Don't list the job you have, but use keywords for the job you're looking for instead. Use exact phrases with correct spelling for the exact job titles that you're applying for.

You can also use keywords in your **About** section. Describe your biggest accomplishments strategically using keywords along the way. You can include sections like "Core Competencies" and "Positions I'm Seeking", then list many keywords beneath them.

Be sure to fill out the **Experience** section. Add any keywords that are relevant to your current job search in the responsibilities of your position. Even if you've never had a job in tech, add something in this section. If you've never had any job, then your job can be "seeking a position in" or "continuing education in", followed by keywords.

Fill out the **Skills** section, keeping your most relevant training at the forefront. If you've had training that isn't relevant to your job search, you may consider omitting it if it's outdated or outside the industry.

5. Not Asking for Recommendations on LinkedIn

Another powerful way to use LinkedIn is as a way to gather positive feedback about your abilities in the tech field.

To start, determine which individuals in your network have seen a demonstration of your skills. Ask them to write you a recommendation. You may also offer to write a recommendation for them in exchange.

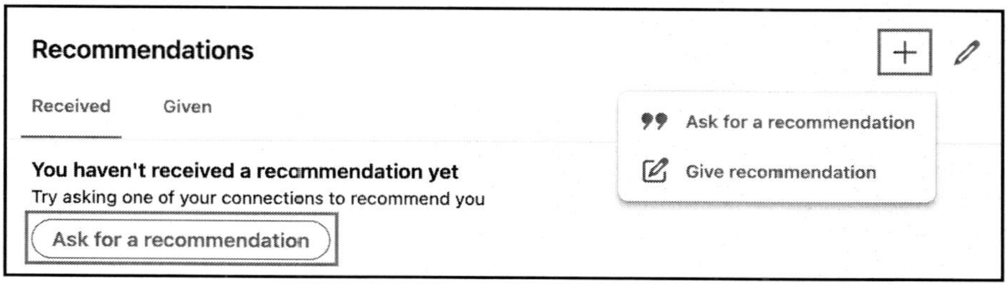

Ask for recommendations on LinkedIn. Be ready to write some in return.

Mentors, former teachers and peers are great people to start asking for recommendations. Also consider any developers you know or anyone you've mentored. This can also include anyone you've volunteered for, any previous companies or coworkers you've had.

Tip: When asking for a recommendation, it's helpful to tell the person exactly what you'd like the recommendation to highlight. You can also include what position you're looking for and suggest wording for the recommendation.

As someone who writes a lot of recommendations, I can say that providing suggested wording can be a real time saver. It ensures that the recommendation meets the needs of the person I'm writing it for. Making it easier to write the recommendation makes it more likely the person you're asking will do it.

Now that you've updated your resume, your cover letter and your LinkedIn profile, it's time to get feedback.

Gathering and Incorporating Feedback

Once you've updated your resume, cover letter and LinkedIn profile, it's time to ask for feedback. A second set of eyes turns up improvements to your application process you'd never think of, like ways to better highlight your skills, new skills to learn or tips to improve your presentation. Plus, hearing other perspectives allows you to see what assumptions employers are making when they read your profile.

Here are some ideas for people to ask:

- Teachers, peers or mentors from your bootcamp or school. If you attended a college or university, they might offer resume assistance.
- New developers who've recently gotten jobs in your industry.
- Engineering team leads or hiring managers in your network who are experienced at evaluating resumes.
- Recruiters. Any time you talk to a recruiter, get feedback while you have them on the line.
- You can use an AI tool like ResumeWorded (https://resumeworded.com/) to check how well your resume matches the skills listed in a job posting.
- Consider hiring a professional resume company to review your material.

Don't forget to ask for feedback on your portfolio as well. Fellow developers might be able to suggest ways to better highlight your skills, new skills to learn or tips to improve your presentation. Research current job descriptions, newsletters and articles to make sure your portfolio contains samples of the latest popular features on your platform.

Once you've gathered the feedback, evaluate it to decide what to use. If it's helpful and constructive, update your materials to incorporate the good advice you got. Just be sure that you keep your resume concise and readable as you incorporate the feedback.

Stepping up Your Game

If you haven't seen the results you wanted yet, it might be time to consider which areas you can put more effort into to increase your chances of success. Even if you followed all the steps in this book, there might be areas you haven't taken full advantage of yet. Here are some ideas for ways to up your game.

Learn New Skills

In tech, it's important to keep expanding your skill set, whether you have a job or not. You might feel like you've just invested a lot in learning skills, but to stay up to date, you need to keep growing.

There are many ways to learn new skills. In Chapter 5, "Traditional & Nontraditional Ways to Find Jobs", you joined a lot of email lists, communities and newsletters. These are great places to learn what's up and coming.

You can also use short courses, tutorials or documentation to learn the latest technology. Some places to find these include:

- Kodeco (https://www.kodeco.com): Use these articles, videos and books to discover the latest in your platform.
- Google Developers Codelabs (https://codelabs.developers.google.com/): Try out and learn the latest features in Google products using the Codelabs. You can also find more learning materials on the main Google Developers (https://developers.google.com/) site.

- Apple's Developer (https://developer.apple.com/whats-new/) site: See what's new at Apple and watch videos, peruse sample code and read developer documentation.
- Medium (https://medium.com): Check out the latest developer blogs on Medium. Many tech bloggers also post accompanying code samples on GitHub.

The best way to learn a new skill is to incorporate it into a new or existing project. You'll find most of your guidance around new features from the vendors' documentation and the platform's communities on Stack Overflow, Reddit, Medium and elsewhere online. Whenever you learn a new skill, be sure to add it to your portfolio.

Expanding Your Network

Your network is the most powerful tool you can use. If you haven't been nurturing this resource, now's the time to pay it some extra attention.

In Chapter 7, "Growing Your Professional Network", you explored many ways to expand your network. How did the process go? Is there anything in this chapter that you could've tried but haven't?

For example:

- If you attended events mostly online, could you potentially find any in person? Or vice versa?
- Are any club meetups or conferences coming up?
- Can you join groups on Facebook, LinkedIn or Reddit that focus on your platform?

Cultivating a network is an ongoing process. In your past attempts, did you find communities that you haven't explored fully yet? Keep digging, and add contacts to your network as you go.

Next, think about the interactions you've had in the past — were there any leads you haven't followed up on? Are there peers from school or bootcamp you haven't connected with yet?

It can feel awkward to connect with people when it's been a while since you met or connected with the person. A great way to break the ice is to boost posts and endorse skills of people you'd like to contact. Look through your network and see if you can answer questions, congratulate successes or engage in conversations. Then, in turn, let your network know about your goals, and they can help you too.

When reconnecting with someone, remind them of when you met and under what circumstances. If you can, think of a reason to talk to them other than making a request. For example, provide some positive feedback on work they've done or a post they've made recently. Then, while catching up, you can inquire about any job leads they may have.

Improving Your Reputation

In Chapter 8, "Building in Public", you explored many ways to enhance your portfolio and put your skills out there for all to see. Now, look for ways you can expand on that work. For instance, if you gave a workshop, could you give it in more places? Could you transform it into a talk? Record it and post it on YouTube? Be sure to reuse what you've created wherever possible.

Next, consider improving what you've made and marketing it to more audiences. For example, turn your project into an article or step-by-step tutorial, then post it on your blog or LinkedIn. Keep adding to your code portfolio. Everything you write adds to your value as a programmer, so market it as widely as you can.

Try to make posting to your blog a regular thing. Use a calendar to map out the posts you want to make a few weeks in advance, so you won't be as likely to skip writing.

Congratulations, you've now gone through the different ways you can refine your job search approach. However, it's not easy to deal with being rejected from one job after another, especially if you get your hopes up each time. Next, you'll learn how to manage your emotions and how to support yourself financially if the search drags on longer than you had budgeted.

Managing Your Emotions During a Challenging Job Search

When your job search doesn't go as planned, it's grueling to keep applying, especially when the perfect companies haven't returned your interest. If you've made it this far in the book, you've invested a lot, so it's painful to not land an interview right away. However, as life coach Steven Redhead said, "The difference between success and failure is not giving up".

Before you start making changes, it's important to make sure you have the right mindset and the financial backing to continue to look for your first tech job.

Dealing With Disappointment

Searching for your first junior developer position is difficult. It puts you through a stressful cycle of hope and disappointment. Know that you're not alone — many job seekers have experienced this. If you're serious about your new career, you must fight to stay positive and stay the course. Here are some ways to do it:

- **Turn rejection into opportunity**: As you're applying for jobs, prepare yourself for rejection. This is hard when the stakes are high and you're feeling financial pressure. Yet, every failed attempt is an opportunity to refine your approach. Try to learn from each application you send and to gather feedback wherever you can.
- **Maintain objectivity**: Your job search might take a long time, but it won't last forever. It's normal that finding the right job takes time, and that doesn't reflect on you as a person. Instead of wasting energy on worrying when you could spend it on more productive things, focus on what you *can* control. Try to remain detached — if you don't raise your hopes too high, they won't have as far to fall.
- **Practice self-care**: Hunting for a job takes a toll on you, so don't neglect your self-care. Engage in activities that rejuvenate you, connect with those who are close to you and find support from other job seekers in the same situation. Be sure to eat well, exercise, sleep and engage in recreation wherever possible. Look for glimmers of hope.
- **Celebrate your progress**: You've already made it through many challenges. Take some time to feel good about all the work you've done. You've grown throughout this process, and you will continue to do so.
- **Remember, it only takes one "yes"**: Keep in mind that it doesn't matter how many times you don't get the interview: You only need one "yes". Even if you experience hundreds of dead ends, it'll all be worth it once that door opens for you.

It's easy to say that you should just keep trying to find the perfect job when money is no issue, but few job seekers have that luxury. If you have financial pressure to find work *soon*, we see you.

Sustaining Your Job Search

To keep job searching, you may have to meet certain financial demands. If landing an interview for a junior dev role is taking longer than expected, you might need to diversify your search — and that's totally OK. Many successful developers took a few detours before getting their first developer job.

In this section, you'll look at alternative roles that can tide you over until you finally land that dream role.

Expanding Your Search

If you aren't finding your perfect tech role right away, a good option is to look for tech-adjacent roles that build your skills and fuel your resume — all while bringing in a paycheck.

Even if these roles aren't the ideal junior dev position, they prepare you for future success. Developers often have a variety of skills and positions before moving into their first developer role.

Some ideas to consider include:

- Data analysis
- Technical writing
- Soft skills
- Networking
- Technical support

These positions might be a way into a company where you can later shift roles onto the developer team. At the very least, they'll make you look better to potential employers.

> **Tip**: Kodeco's article, Earn While You Learn: 5 Tech Jobs for New Coders (https://www.kodeco.com/34627370-earn-while-you-learn-5-tech-jobs-for-new-coders) discusses roles that can boost your resume in more detail.

Depending on your situation, you may consider something other than a full-time role. You'll look at those next.

Alternatives to Full-Time Jobs

If you're having trouble finding the perfect dev job, you might consider bringing in money to sustain your search with a part-time role or a paid internship. Both of these will supplement your income and help you gain experience.

Particularly with internships, you want to be careful to avoid roles that take up your time without giving you what you need. Even internships should be fairly compensated. Avoid unpaid internships.

Also, make sure that the company is giving you opportunities to learn and grow. When you interview for the position, take the opportunity to learn about the company's commitment to mentorship and leadership. These are critical to having a good internship.

It can be difficult to find part-time roles or mentorships. These roles are oftentimes not advertised, particularly with large companies. You'll need to be proactive in searching for these roles.

Some ideas for finding these roles include:

- Ask companies directly if they have part-time roles or internships available.
- Utilize your network for tips and referrals.
- If you're a recent graduate, your school's career center might have information about internship opportunities.
- Check job boards, including internship-focused sites like WayUp (https://www.wayup.com/).

Now that you've considered some ways to make your search more sustainable, look at your expectations to make sure they're serving you.

Remember that building a career in tech is a lot like building an app: It's an iterative process that involves testing.

You're nearly done now! To wrap up, try to apply a developer mindset to your job search.

Implementing a Continuous Improvement Process for Your Job Search

Keep in mind that preparing to get a job isn't a one-and-done task — it's a journey. You can think of your job hunt like an app: You don't simply publish an app and ignore it. You use feedback to improve it. You incorporate the latest technology to optimize it. You look for new ways to market it and find a bigger audience. Your job search works the same way.

If that's frustrating, remember that you'll learn and grow through this process. You have already done a lot of correct things to start your job search. If it's not yielding results, try augmenting your approach. If, for some reason, you're stuck, don't give up. Try to find the piece that's not working or try another approach. You'll soon improve this skill, just as you improved your coding skills.

Even if you're facing a challenging job market, don't get discouraged. That just means the search may take more time and effort — it doesn't mean it's impossible. A ZipRecruiter survey (https://www.ziprecruiter.com/blog/laid-off-tech-workers/) found that after the massive tech layoffs in 2022, 78% of the people who were laid off found a new job within just three months. That's despite massive competition from the thousands of people who were suddenly searching for new roles at the same time.

If there aren't a lot of opportunities at this moment, use this time to keep adding to your resume, refining your portfolio and building your skills and network. Soon, you'll find the interview you seek. Success is a combination of having your skills on display while meeting an opportunity. Keep putting yourself out there and improving your presentation, and an opportunity will come your way.

Adjust your expectations to be as realistic as you can, but keep your eyes on the prize and have hope. Anything that's worth doing is usually a challenge, and you'll rise to this one. After all, you learned to code, you'll nail this, too.

Resources

- Tips for Getting a Software Developer Internship (https://dev.to/simonholdorf/tips-for-getting-a-software-developer-internship-p31) gives you suggestions for how to pursue an internship while working toward a full-time position.
- Software Developer Cover Letter (https://www.betterteam.com/software-developer-cover-letter) has some great links that can help you make your cover letters specific and effective for each job you apply for.
- Are You Using the Top Keywords for Your LinkedIn in 2023? (https://www.letseatgrandma.com/blog/top-keywords-for-linkedin-2021/) is a guide to LinkedIn keywords that'll help you optimize your profile to come up in searches related to the job you're seeking.

Key Takeaways

- The job search can be a daunting process, but you can overcome the challenge — it only takes one "yes".
- The market can ebb and flow — revise your expectations if needed, and keep trying.
- There can be many steps between where you are and where you want to be — any step toward your goal is the right direction.
- Getting a job is like any other skill — you improve through practice.
- Feedback is a valuable tool to refine your approach and perfect your resume, LinkedIn and portfolio.

Action Plan

- **Review your application materials** and make sure that they show your strengths, are up to date, are easy to read and are free of typos.
- **Identify three people** that could act as mentors on your journey. Reach out to them to review your application materials.
- Ask one developer from your network to **provide feedback on your portfolio**.
- **Identify one job search strategy** you haven't utilized yet that you can put into action.
- **Research one cutting-edge skill** that you can learn and add to your portfolio.

> **Reflect on what you've learned**: Find this chapter's worksheet (PDF (https://github.com/kodecocodes/booh-materials/blob/editions/1.0/10-what-to-do-if-you-are-still-not-landing-interviews/Chapter10Worksheet.pdf)) in this book's GitHub materials repo.

11 Conclusion

Whew — from deciding whether now's the time to jump into a job search to figuring out what you want and need from a position; from preparing your materials to growing your network and staying fresh with your tech learning — this book's taken you along your first steps in your mobile dev job search! Thank you for trusting us to join you on this journey. Know that we're rooting for you every step of the way as you land your first interview — and all the ones that follow.

We encourage you to return to this book from time to time, whether to reflect on where you want to go next in your career or simply to enrich your networking, learning and sharing skills. Just because this is a job search book doesn't mean you can *only* use it when you're searching.

We recommend revisiting the worksheets too. If you use these over time, you can look back and see how your thoughts, feelings and approaches have evolved.

Kodeco offers a growing number of professional development resources, including the following articles and video course of special interest to job seekers:

- How to Write the Perfect Resume After Graduating a Coding Bootcamp (https://www.kodeco.com/36875585-how-to-write-the-perfect-resume-after-graduating-a-coding-bootcamp) by Jay Strawn. Combine the advice here with Chapter 4, "Creating a Resume & Portfolio", to create the ultimate standout application materials.

- Mock Interview Techniques for Tech Job Searchers (https://www.kodeco.com/34421990-mock-interview-techniques-for-tech-job-searchers) by Lea Marolt Sonnenschein offers detailed advice to help you get ready for the interviews you land.

- The Acing the iOS Interview (https://www.kodeco.com/25254417-acing-the-ios-interview) video course by Lea Marolt Sonnenschein walks aspiring iOS developers through what to expect in technical interviews.
- Evaluating Job Offers: How to Decide If a Company Is Right for You (https://www.kodeco.com/36309982-evaluating-job-offers-how-to-decide-if-a-company-is-right-for-you) by Jeff Rames. Ideally, you'll work through this article before you're in the thick of the hunt so you can define your priorities before you need to compare offers. Regardless of when you put this to use, you'll find it an excellent resource to logically evaluate next steps.

If you have any questions or comments as you work through this book, please stop by our forums at https://forums.kodeco.com and look for this book's forum category.

Thank you again for purchasing this book. Your continued support is what makes the books, tutorials, videos and other things we do at Kodeco possible. We truly appreciate it!

– The *Hack Your Job Search* team

Made in United States
North Haven, CT
10 November 2026

22071057R00104